The Wealthy Woman

A man is not a financial plan

The Wealthy Woman

A man is not a financial plan

A Woman's Guide to Achieving Financial Security

Mary Waring

Chartered Accountant
Fellow of the Institute of Chartered Accountants in England and Wales

Chartered Financial Planner
Fellow of the Personal Finance Society

First published and distributed in the United Kingdom in 2014 by
Wealth For Women Publishing, Surrey

A catalogue record of this book is available from the British Library.
ISBN: 978-0-9927028-0-9

First published in the United Kingdom in 2014

Cover design by Truly Ace www.trulyace.com
Produced in the UK by Shore Books and Design. www.shore-books.co.uk

To my darling mum, who unwittingly and unknowingly
provided the inspiration for this book.

Praise for
The Wealthy Woman - A man is not a financial plan

"I believe that a lot of women put their heads in the sand where their financial planning is concerned. Well, get yours out now and read Mary's book. It's a straightforward, no-nonsense approach to a subject that a lot of us find a little bit daunting. It'll make you think and realise that, with a little planning you, too, could be on the road to an optimistic financial future."

Annie Brooks, Director, Sister Snog

"A thoroughly informative read. Enlightening whatever your circumstances, Mary's style speaks volumes and reaches out to those of us who are number phobic!"

Camilla Choudhury -Khawaja, The Women's Lawyer

"Mary, if your book is not a bestseller I'll eat my hat! Well thought out, great story telling, thought provoking, funny, all combined with great advice delivered in an easy to understand way without being patronising. Wish I'd had it years ago and it should definitely be on the school curriculum!"

Barbara Cosgrave, Business Style Expert

"Mary is a well-respected and trusted Financial Adviser and her book gives sound advice and insights in an easily accessible way. It makes you think, it makes you smile and will help you on your way to a brighter financial future".

Elaine Hickmott, Business Alchemist

"In life we have many relationships. This book will show you how to have a beautiful love affair with money that'll turn you into a wealthy woman."

Hela Wozniak-Kay, Director Sister Snog

What this book will show you

This book will guide you on your journey to become a wealthy woman by showing you how taking small steps on a regular basis can lead to a significant increase in your wealth.

"Wealthy" will mean different things to different women. It doesn't necessarily mean "rolling in it" and having so much money that you'll enter *The Times* 'rich list'. It may simply mean you feel confident you will have enough money to do the things that you plan to do in the future, no matter how lavish or frugal a lifestyle you lead.

For some, it will mean financial freedom so you no longer have to work. For others, it will mean you no longer panic during the last week of the month that your income is about to run out.

If you currently have such a lack of control over your finances that you are too afraid to open your credit card statement at the end of the month, this book will show you how to take control.

"The Wealthy Woman" will encourage you to think about your attitude towards money and your relationship with it.

The subject of money raises a huge number of different emotions. Many women love it and enjoy it, whilst many others fear it. It's not money itself that is important, it's what you do with it that counts.

> *"Money is only a tool. It will take you wherever you wish, but it will not replace you as the driver..." Ayn Rand (1957)[1]*

It's easy to be wealthy just as it's easy to be poor. There's very little difference in the way you can become either. You are in a position where you can improve your wealth. Whatever your dreams and aspirations around money, there is nothing to stop you moving towards those dreams.

---

1 Rand, A. (1957). *Atlas Shrugged*. Ayn Rand Center. Retrieved 25 August 2013 from http://www.aynrand.org/site/News2?id=7429

Contents

Acknowledgments

A large number of people have provided me with help and advice to get my first book published. As always, when you take on any new task you experience a great mixture of both excitement and trepidation. Therefore, to all of you who have helped me, I owe you a debt of gratitude.

A few people deserve a special mention:

Tom Evans was instrumental in encouraging me to undertake the project at least a year before I had initially planned. He made the process sound so simple and straightforward that I decided there was no reason not to start. His encouragement was the impetus I needed. So thank you for that, Tom.

Several friends have read the manuscript and provided invaluable feedback. Thanks to **Annie Brooks, Camilla Choudhury-Khawaja, Barbara Cosgrave, Elaine Hickmott and Hela Wozniak-Kay.** You are all fantastic women and I'm delighted to know you. Please hurry up and get your own book completed, each of you, so I can return the favour.

A quick thank you, as well, to **Karen Skidmore, Tricia Woolfrey** and **Karen Williams.** Each of these fabulous women have already been through the book publishing process and provided very useful advice and encouragement. I really appreciate the time you spent with me discussing the various options.

Finally, a huge thank you to my husband, **Tony Waring.** Hopefully, now the book is finished I will no longer be spending so much time in my office, and I won't be editing a book on my next holiday!

Thank you all for your help and support.

Mary Waring

The Wealthy Woman
A man is not a financial plan
An overview

"There are people who have money and people who are rich..." -
Coco Chanel

I frequently hear women tell me that they struggle with maths and don't understand finance. If I had £1 for every woman who said to me "I don't do maths", I'd be a millionaire. I exaggerate - of course I wouldn't be a millionaire, because I don't know a million women! But, I would have accumulated a fair pot of £1 coins.

Does "I don't do maths", "I don't have a clue about my finances" feel and sound familiar to you? If so, you're not alone.

Many women appear to have a real mental block when it comes to finance and maths. This isn't due to lack of education, or lack of common sense. I hear these comments from very clever, bright, articulate, sensible women, who are working at the highest level within their profession.

Yet, despite their level of education, despite how much they have achieved in their chosen professions and their careers, these women are convinced they can't do maths. A coach working on limiting beliefs would have a field day with these women.

If you're bright enough to be a scientist, doctor, lawyer, bring up a family of three kids and manage to get them all to the right school/ right football practice/right ballet lesson at the right time, then you're actually bright enough to get to grips with your finances.

Don't be intimidated by financial advisers who talk jargon and convince you it's all terribly complicated. Of course, some of it is, because otherwise we wouldn't need to study and pass all the exams we have to take.

Understanding some of the basics and feeling more comfortable around finances is straight forward, *if only someone would show you how!*

Is it just women who feel this way about their finances, and not men?

Maybe the more relevant question to consider would be: is it just women who <u>admit</u> to feeling this way? Who knows? We women are often very skilled at concentrating on our faults and weaknesses and listing all the things we can't do, rather than thinking about our strengths, our achievements and listing all the things that we can do.

What really interests me is <u>why</u> do so many women believe that they can't do maths and that they're not good with finances?

I went to an all girls' school at secondary level, so have no idea whether I would have been taught differently if I had been at a mixed school. Maybe, the way maths is generally taught is more suited to a male way of learning, rather than a female preference. Men and women do have different brains, and learn differently. After all, we all know men are from Mars and women are from Venus!

Maybe, women are generally better at the more artistic and creative subjects. If so, I'm definitely one of the exceptions, since I loved maths at school, and cannot draw even if my life depended on it. I got 26% in my art exam at age 14 and decided to give it up at that stage, since I realised it just wasn't for me.

My background

My interest in maths is, I guess, because I've got a very logical brain and love to follow a process. To me, maths is very black and white. It's either right or it's wrong, and this really appeals to me. In my world, two plus two always equals four, and there are no exceptions to this rule. I love the true clarity of this.

I studied business studies at university, specialising in accountancy, and trained and worked as a chartered accountant once I had my degree. I was employed as a finance director up until 2005, when I decided I wanted to do something different. I wanted to experience the world of the self-employed, so I could be in charge of my own future.

At that time, my aim was to reduce my working hours and I had dreams of working a three-day week, with lots of time off and fun holidays.

However, that nirvana of working a short week has not yet happened. All of a sudden, when I was working for myself rather than someone else, I became so focussed on growing my business that I've worked much longer hours than I've ever worked as an employee. And believe me, I often worked long hours as a finance director.

When I became self-employed, I initially trained as a mortgage adviser and, luckily, I did experience the huge boom in the property market during 2006 and 2007. My business was expanding significantly and I wondered why on earth I hadn't taken the plunge to be self-employed many years earlier.

However, as we all know, what goes up must come down! The property market then collapsed and my business suffered significantly.

In short, I've had an interest and aptitude for maths from a very early age and I've been involved in finance ever since I left university - about a million years ago now! At least, so it seems on some days.

I had always considered that at some future date I would train as an Independent Financial Adviser (IFA). However, whilst my mortgage business was so successful I didn't have the time or, indeed, the inclination at that stage, to do the hundreds of hours worth of additional study and exams.

The drop in my business levels, and therefore the additional time I now had available, gave me the impetus I needed to go back to the hard slog of studying to achieve my IFA qualification. I completed my studies in 2010.

When I first became an adviser I was surprised at how few females there were in the profession. Figures state only about 10% of advisers are female. The typical adviser is male, middle aged, grey hair and grey suit.

Whilst there's absolutely nothing wrong with that, it made me wonder whether that's why so many women are not dealing with their finances. Is it because they don't have enough rapport with the typical adviser and don't feel that he is the right person to help them?

As a result, I decided to specialise in advice to women, since I realised there's a large number of women out there who maybe aren't getting the advice they need and want.

I certainly don't believe that men aren't capable of giving advice to women; of course they are. After all, recommendations as to what to do with your money are equally relevant whatever your gender. However, maybe women aren't seeking advice because the whole profession doesn't appear to be particularly female friendly.

As the more caring, sharing gender, it's interesting that more women aren't entering the financial services profession. After all, it's about talking to people, asking them about themselves and asking them about their future aims, hopes, goals and dreams. In fact, isn't this what we do every day when we sit down to chat with our friends and colleagues?

In my experience, women frequently don't feel totally comfortable about finances and don't really know where to go to get advice from someone they trust.

If that is the case, then I hope this book can go some way to filling that gap. I hope it can help you to feel more comfortable with your finances and encourage you to take more responsibility and control.

This book is designed as a basic introduction to understanding and taking control of your finances. It's not a get rich quick scheme, and certainly won't promise to make you a millionaire overnight. If that's what you were expecting, then I'm afraid you're going to be sorely disappointed. And probably fed up that you shelled out cash for it and have immediately made a dent in your plans to be a millionaire.

It's also not going to tell you which specific stocks and shares to invest in to increase your wealth, or how to design an investment portfolio. The whole area of how to choose what to do with your money is a totally separate topic in itself, and outside the scope of this book.

What this book will do is explain the basics, so that you can start to feel comfortable about money and no longer feel that it's an area to be ignored or feared.

Most things can be easily understood once they've been explained properly. That's what this book is designed to do. After all, it's not rocket science. It's just a case of knowing how you put yourself in a situation where you can understand your financial position and then take the necessary steps to start improving your financial future.

It's a process for you to follow to determine exactly where your finances are now, and what small steps can be taken on a regular basis to improve them.

There's no magic formula, just a system broken down into individual steps for you to follow.

At the end of each chapter there is a recap of the main area covered, and then some action steps for you to take.

Reading this book on its own will do nothing to improve your wealth if you don't do anything with what you've learnt.

You need to be fully engaged with the process, so that it becomes a habit.

Reading and understanding what you've read isn't enough: you need to make decisions and take massive action.

The exercises will allow you to get and feel comfortable with your wealth and understand what you can do to improve it. Even if you believe you've totally understood what you've just read and can complete the action points, do make sure you do them anyway.

This book is about taking the small steps necessary to improve your wealth. If you don't start on the exercises, the chances are the book will have been an interesting read (hopefully!), but won't actually have had any impact on you and your future financial position.

Your journey to being a wealthy woman requires action on a consistent and regular basis.

How to read this book

Everyone assimilates knowledge in a different way, so it's up to you to decide what method of working through the book will provide you with the greatest benefit.

Maybe, you want to stop at the end of each chapter and do the exercises in full before moving on to the next chapter. Maybe, you want to read the book through fully to start with and then go back and do the exercises. Perhaps you want to jump straight in at a particular chapter and not necessarily read the book in order.

Choose whatever route is going to work best for you and give you the greatest benefit. Do remember that, to get benefit from the book, you do need to make sure you complete the action steps.

I've left several blank pages at the end of the book for note taking. That way you can start the exercises as you go along. You now don't have any excuse not to!

Updates

My aim has been to make the book as generic as possible and not dependent on specific tax rules and regulations. However, there are certain instances in the book where figures or rules are quoted, which may change over time. To ensure the book is always up to date, there will be a specific page on my website to update the figures and rules following legislative changes.

All figures quoted in this book are based on the tax rules in effect during the tax year 2013/14. See www.mary-waring.co.uk/TheWW-updates/ for updated figures in subsequent years.

I'd love to get your feedback. Please do let me know how you get on. Email me at Mary@mary-waring.co.uk to let me know what you liked, what worked for you, and whether you had any "ah-ha" moments from it. Tell me when you find the little nugget of information in this book that really hits the spot for you.

If you didn't like it, I'd be interested to know that, too. Tell me why it didn't work for you and what you would have preferred. Constructive feedback is really useful. Do be gentle with me though, please, since I'm a sensitive soul!

Here's what you're going to cover on your journey through the book:

Chapter 1: Because you're worth it

Chapter 1 looks at all the competing priorities there are on your income during your 20s, 30s and 40s. These competing priorities will always exist. As a result, it's not enough to decide to save whatever amount of money you have left at the end of the month. This is because, guess what? You're unlikely to have anything left in your bank account at the end of the month.

Saving and improving your finances can't be passive. You have to make a decision to improve your financial position and take action to achieve it.

Chapter 2: A stitch in time

Chapter 2 looks at how the decisions you make about what to do with your money in your 20s, 30s and 40s impacts on the lifestyle you lead when you're older.

It's never too late to take control of your finances, but the earlier you start financial planning, the easier it will be to achieve your long term goal.

Chapter 3: Don't be an ostrich

Chapter 3 looks at what is likely to happen to you if you don't take the necessary action to improve your wealth. There are many ways to fool yourself it will all be okay. However, the best way to <u>know</u> it will be okay is to stop making excuses or relying on others, and take responsibility yourself.

Chapter 4: And we're off

Chapter 4 shows how to calculate your net worth: what you own, less what you owe. This is your starting point and you use this to see how much improvement you have made over time.

The chapter then goes on to show you how to set your goal for what you want your net worth to increase to in the future.

Chapter 5: Till debt us do part

Chapter 5 shows how important it is to be in control of your debt - all types of debt: credit card, mortgage, loans, and overdraft.

The important thing to look at is how much you pay back in total over the life of the debt, not how much you pay back each month.

The less you repay each month, the longer it will take to get the debt fully paid off, and the greater the total interest charge. The important thing to consider is how quickly you can get any debt repaid.

Be warned now, the figures will shock you!

Chapter 6: Getting interesting

Chapter 6 shows how saving even a small amount over a sustained period can really add up to a sensible sum. Yes, of course the more you can save each month the better. However, don't be put off by the fact the amount you're saving may appear too small to bother with. Keep on keeping on, and you'll see a difference.

Chapter 7: In out, in out, shake it all about

Chapter 7 deals with the fact that, before you can control your spending and start to increase savings, you need to know exactly what your hard-earned cash is currently being spent on.

The chapter shows you how to monitor all your cash flows - both money that flows in and money that flows out.

Small changes in spending or income, applied consistently over a long period, can really make a difference. Don't worry, I'm not going to suggest you increase your working hours. This is all about working smarter, not harder.

Chapter 8: Getting started, not too taxing

As previously mentioned, this book is designed to be a generic look at how to improve your finances, regardless of what country you live in or what the tax laws are. However, for those living in the UK, Chapter 8 will provide further details about pensions and individual savings accounts (ISAs), and how each of these can be used to move you onwards in your journey to be a wealthy woman.

Chapter 9: Wealthy woman wobbles

Despite your best efforts and best intentions, things do not always go according to plan. Everything in this book is a long-term plan: a process to follow that will move you in the right direction up the wealth ladder.

Chapter 9 looks at what can go wrong on your journey and how you can deal with it.

Chapter 10: The new you

Chapter 10 will ensure you finish this book on a real high. It will show you how much you've achieved by following the steps and processes discussed in the book.

If you follow all the advice, you can't help but have improved your financial position. You will no longer be burying your head in the sand, or fooling yourself things will all be okay. You will have a plan in place and be on track to reach your goal.

Congratulations, you are now on your way to being a wealthy woman!

Chapter 1: Because you're worth it

"Everyone wants to ride with you in the limo, but what you want is someone who will take the bus with you when the limo breaks down..." - Oprah Winfrey

This book is relevant for you whatever your age, marital status, income or education. Never think that you are too old, or too young, to start to do something to improve you finances - and to be in greater control of your wealth.

Of course, it's common sense that the earlier you start saving the better. If you start saving at age 20, all other things being equal, you will save more over your working life than if you delay saving until you reach 50.

At each stage of your life you will have different priorities and different objectives. A basic understanding of your finances, how to budget and how to improve your wealth, will be relevant whatever your age and whatever it is you want to achieve with your money.

Unfortunately, you often don't recognise the value of starting to save at an early age until you are older, and then you can only think, "I wish I'd started saving sooner."

If you had a crystal ball and could look into the future, this would help. I can't provide a crystal ball and cannot tell the future. However, what I can do is use my experience as an Independent Financial Adviser (IFA) and tell you some stories of the women I've spoken to at different stages of their life. I can tell you how their attitude to money either shapes their future or, depending on their age, is shaped by the actions they took (or didn't take) at an earlier age.

These stories will be related by following two women through their lifetimes, "Savvy Sarah" and "Not-so-savvy Nicola". Savvy Sarah makes sensible decisions about her finances and her future wealth, which provides a good grounding for the lifestyle she will lead in later years.

However, for every savvy woman who takes the correct action, there is likely to be a not-so-savvy woman who doesn't take correct action or, more commonly, takes the absolutely incorrect action.

Not-so-savvy Nicola makes decisions, which seem correct for her at the time, but with hindsight, may have been a bit short sighted.

I will show you in more detail the typical financial priorities each of these women face in their 20s, 30s, and 40s.

All the details are based on actual client examples and are designed to be representative of the type of financial priorities you will have during each decade of your life.

By relating these experiences as those of either Savvy Sarah or Not-so-savvy Nicola, I can tell you the real life stories of my clients without identifying any of them specifically.

Whilst you read through the following, see whether your actions are more aligned with those of Sarah or Nicola.

Of course, these are only broad examples and your specifics may be very different. Hopefully, however, and depending on your age, you will recognise yourself, your daughter, granddaughter, or friends in the following.

You're in your 20s

You're probably earning a reasonable basic salary, but have little extra cash for saving. Chances are that, regardless of your cash position, you have little incentive to save for your future and your retirement. Let's face it, at this age you're probably hoping you're going to retire reasonably wealthy at age 50.

You haven't got a plan, yet, as to how to achieve this, but you know you're not going to be one of those women who have to keep working until they drop because they haven't saved enough money at a younger age. You're much too smart for that. However, since you're only in your 20s, there's plenty of time to start saving. You may as well put that on the back burner for now, and start thinking about it tomorrow.

Besides, you've got a student loan to pay off. You also want to keep up to date with the latest fashions and enjoy shopping at the weekend with your girlfriends. You work hard during the week, so you deserve a bit of a treat every now and then. That's not too much to ask, is it?

Yes, you know you need to get round to saving at some point, but you've got what appears to be a whole lifetime ahead of you until you reach retirement age. You may as well wait for a few years before you start to worry about that.

However, maybe now's the <u>best</u> time to start saving

<u>Let's take a look at the two different women in their 20s.</u>

Savvy Sarah has seen her mother and grandmother struggle with finances and not have enough money. She's determined things will be different for her, so she decides to start saving now. Not a lot, because she doesn't have much disposable income at this stage, but she's keen to get started.

She decides to save £25 a month into an investment plan, since she wants to get into good habits at an early age regarding her financial future. She spends more than that a week on clothes and make up without thinking twice about it, so £25 a month is doable with a little bit of planning and commitment.

If she continues to save this amount for 40 years and receives a return of 5% a year, the amount saved at the end of that 40-year period will be worth around £38,000.

This is never going to be enough to give her a comfortable lifestyle. Sarah realises this. However, the other things that Savvy Sarah knows are:

- If she starts saving £25 a month now when she's in her 20s, over time that monthly savings amount will increase as her salary increases. As a result, the final figure for her savings pot will be much higher than £38,000.

- The amount she's actually paid in by saving £25 a month for 40 years is £12,000. It's cost her £12,000, but is actually worth £38,000. This increase has been gained through the 5% investment growth each year.

When she looks at it this way, £38,000 seems a very nice return for an investment that has cost her £12,000 over time.

Just imagine what the final figure will be if she increases the monthly payment.

Compare this to **Not-so-savvy Nicola**, who didn't start saving in her 20s, but instead waited another 10 years to start. Rather than the 40 years Sarah had, Nicola now has 30 years to save, if she plans to retire in her mid 60s.

If Nicola also saves £25 a month, over the 30 years she will save £9,000. This is three-quarters of the amount saved by Sarah.

On this basis, presumably at the end of 30 years Nicola's pot will be three-quarters of the size of Sarah's pot?

In fact, after 30 years, using a return of 5% a year, Nicola's fund will then be worth just short of £21,000. Compared to Sarah's pot of £38,000, Nicola's pot is worth just over half.

How can it be that Nicola saved three-quarters of the amount saved by Sarah, but her pot was worth nowhere near three-quarters of the value of Sarah's pot? In fact it was worth just over half of Sarah's.

There are two reasons for this. Firstly, Nicola saved less money than Sarah since she started her saving plan 10 years later. Secondly, Nicola's savings pot had 10 years less investment growth than Sarah's.

For each year the money is invested, both Sarah and Nicola earned interest on the amount saved, - and also earned interest on the interest. Earning interest on interest is referred to as "compounding". Sarah had the benefit of compounding for 10 years more than Nicola.

We'll look at this issue of compound growth in more detail in Chapter 6 "Getting interesting".

At this stage, the message to take from the example of Savvy Sarah and Not-so-savvy Nicola is that it's never too early to start saving for your future.

Even if it's only a very small amount, it will set up a savings habit. The important thing is to start. As Nike says, "Just do it". Get a standing order in place, so that money automatically goes out of your bank account on a set day each month into some form of savings plan.

Once you've started saving, it becomes an easier decision to increase the monthly amount. The longer you delay before you start saving, the more you need to put in each month to get to the same end figure. Then, as a result, the harder it becomes to start saving because you need to find a larger sum each month. It's a vicious circle.

Therefore, if you're in your 20s and think retirement seems too far off to worry about, ask yourself:

Do you want to be like Savvy Sarah or like Not-so-savvy Nicola?

Can you cut back on your spending on clothes, make up, socialising, or whatever it is your money goes on, to find at least a small sum to start building your wealth?

If you're not convinced yet, read on to see what you are likely to experience in later years if you don't start early.

You're in your 30s

You're feeling very grown up and mature at this stage and have decided you'll buy a property. You recognise that the mortgage repayment won't be significantly different from the rent you're paying. You think it's much better, therefore, to be paying that money towards a flat that belongs to you, rather than paying it to a landlord.

You've now got to think about saving enough money for a deposit. Some of your friends have wealthy parents who have helped their children out by contributing significantly towards the money they need. However, your parents don't have the savings to be able to help out. Instead, it's all down to you.

You haven't been a big saver in your 20s, so the thought of now having to take control of, and manage, your money is a bit scary. You know, though, that you need to get started if you ever want to get your foot on the property ladder.

You're hoping that saving for your deposit will set up some good savings habits, which you plan to continue after you've bought the house.

You recognise that, by the time you've paid the deposit, associated legal fees and spent money to furnish the place, you'll be feeling quite penniless. Money will probably be a bit tight to start with but, once you've got used to paying a mortgage, you'll be able to plan your spending. That way there'll be some money left over to put into a savings plan for the future.

Let's take a look at the two different women in their 30s.

Savvy Sarah is very keen to own her own property. Her rented flat is okay, but she's sharing with two other friends to keep the cost down and, sometimes, she just wishes she had a bit more privacy.

She doesn't mind if it's a small flat, even a studio will do, provided it's all hers. She received a small inheritance from her grandmother a few years ago. Not a huge amount, but enough to get her started with a savings plan. Since then, she's added to it each month, a small bit at a time.

Whenever Savvy Sarah receives a pay rise or a bonus she makes sure that some of the extra money goes into her savings plan. She now knows that if she cuts back on one night out a week, and saves the amount that she would have spent, she will have enough money for her deposit in two years time.

Yes, sometimes when she stays in instead of being out socialising with her friends, she wonders if she's doing the right thing. However, generally she knows it's more important for her to be able to buy her own property than to go out and have the effects of yet another late night to cope with the next day.

Compare this to **Not-so-savvy Nicola**. She also received a small inheritance from her grandmother a few years ago. She had intended to save some of it, but having paid off her credit card bill, had a smashing holiday with her friends, and bought some new clothes, there didn't seem to be enough left to bother saving. She ended up spending it all.

The money is now all gone, and Nicola's not quite sure what on earth it was spent on. Worse than that, her credit card bill is back up at its limit again, even though she used the inheritance to pay it all off just a few years ago. How did that happen?

Like Sarah, Nicola also rents but, unlike Sarah, Nicola rents quite an expensive one-bed apartment, since she doesn't want to share. She recognises that the amount of rent she's paying is a huge chunk of her income, but just accepts that this is what she needs to pay for the lifestyle she likes and wants.

Nicola would love to buy her own place, but can't see how that's going to happen, at least not in the short term. Hopefully, she'll meet someone soon and get married. Let's hope he's stinking rich and owns a decent apartment she can move in to.

She has been told, "A man is not a financial plan," but in the absence of any plan of her own it will have to do... at least for now!

You're in your 40s

You've been married for several years now and have two adorable young children. For a short period after having the children you went back to your job in the corporate world. However, you paid such extortionate childcare fees, you've realised there wasn't enough left over at the end of the month to warrant what you missed out on by working such long hours.

You've come to the conclusion that having young children and corporate life doesn't really mix and so you've decided to become self-employed to give you the flexibility you need to look after your family.

However, earning anywhere near the income you earned as an employee is proving harder than you thought, especially when your working hours are limited by childcare. Luckily, your partner earns a decent salary, so with the two incomes combined you're doing okay.

Still, there are huge demands on your income - mainly property and education. You're wondering whether you can afford to move to a bigger property, so there's more room for your growing family. The family home that was plenty big enough for the two of you, is now feeling quite cramped with two young children and all their accompanying toys and paraphernalia. How can two small children take up so much space?

You're hoping the children will get into the good local state school, but if they don't you're going to consider paying for private education. You went to the local state school yourself, but know that educational standards in a number of state schools are different these days and, of course, you do want what's best for your kids. Who wouldn't?

You're not sure whether you can afford to, especially considering that long term you would also like to assist them with university costs.

In an ideal world, you won't end up paying for their school education, since there's a good chance they'll get into the local state school. However, you want to have a plan for this option, just in case.

<u>Let's look at the two different women in their 40s</u>

Savvy Sarah has always been careful with money. She and her partner, Sam, have a reasonably low mortgage in relation to the value of their property, and so can always benefit from the most competitive rates that are available.

Sarah reduced her working hours following the birth of her children. As soon as her income reduced, she reduced her spending to match. She's always been very task orientated and therefore decided to treat managing her income the same way as she would any other work project.

She managed several staff and huge budgets when she was department manager, so managing her personal finances should be a doddle. She's determined that, even though her income has reduced, she should still keep up her savings plan. It has meant that she and Sam don't always go out to the swankiest restaurants and sometimes choose to eat in, instead.

Sometimes, they don't always have the holidays they would like to have if money was no object and they have to choose a cheaper option. However, the important thing to both of them is that they take time away together as a family and have fun.

As a result, Sarah knows that if the children don't get into the local state school (but, fingers crossed that they do), she does have a sum of money set aside that will cover a significant chunk of the cost of private education.

If she doesn't have to dip into this to cover primary or secondary school it should be quite a tidy sum when her youngest hits university age. That gives great comfort that she can afford for both children to attend university, if that's what they want when they get to that age.

Compare this to **Not-so-savvy Nicola**. She also reduced her working hours following the birth of her children. However, she didn't think to reduce her spending as well. Honestly, it just didn't occur to her.

She has always been one to "keep up with the Joneses," so insists that the family holiday at whatever location is the must see "hotspot" for the year. Luckily for her, Nicola's partner, Nathan, also thinks it's important to show off how much he earns - even though his earnings have fallen significantly over recent years with the downturn in the economy.

Appearance is everything. "Fake it, till you make it", is Nathan's motto, and it's served him well up to now.

The family have frequently holidayed with their neighbours, Mr and Mrs Jones. Mr Jones earns significantly more than Nathan, so Nicola and Nathan have struggled to afford the lifestyle they lead.

But, hey, what are credit cards for if it's not to have a lovely holiday with your closest friends a few times a year?

If Nicola's children don't get into the local state school they will really struggle to afford private schooling. But, she'd choose that option over sending them to the school they may be allocated as second choice.

Let's hope it never comes to that.

Sometimes the worry is enough to keep Nicola awake at night and she wishes she and Nathan were each a bit more sensible with money. As soon as there's any spare money in the bank they go out for a slap up meal to one of the more trendy (i.e. expensive) restaurants in central London. She loves seeing the look on her neighbour's face when she tells Mrs Jones where they went and how much it cost.

Since they only go to exclusive restaurants, they often see celebrities there. Nicola loves being part of this crowd: although she recognises eating at the same restaurant doesn't really make her part of the crowd. It just makes her an onlooker.

It also emphasises just how little money she and Nathan have in relation to the celebrities and other people who tend to frequent these places. Some of these earn much more in a week than Nathan earns in a whole year. Surely, that can't be fair!

Nicola does recognise that they have to change their spending habits. However, it's quite difficult, because the social set she's part of doesn't seem to have been affected by the economy in the same way she has.

She's certainly not going to draw attention to their precarious financial position by refusing invitations to evenings out, no matter how much the evening costs.

Maybe Nathan should try to get a new job which offers a higher salary. That's probably easier than cutting back on their spending.

She's going to book a table tonight at the rather chichi restaurant that just opened last week to discuss this plan with him, and see what he thinks.

The decisions that Sarah and Nicola have taken in their 20s, 30s and 40s has a significant influence on the lifestyle they each lead at a later age. The following chapter will continue to look at their lives as they move on in years and how they are shaped by the decisions they've taken up to now.

If you are dealing with your money in a similar way to Savvy Sarah, then well done. You're well on the way to setting up good financial habits for the future, which will benefit you in later years.

If you recognise your habits are more similar to those of Not-so-savvy Nicola, then the good news is - you're in good company. There are many, many women like this. The bad news is - if you don't change your habits and your relationship with money, you're going to be in for a rocky ride in later years. Don't worry if you do fall into this category. There are a number of ways to address this, which will be dealt with in subsequent chapters.

What you've covered

What this chapter has shown you is that, regardless of whether you are in your 20s, 30s or 40s, there will always be competing priorities on your income.

Don't assume that as you get older - and hopefully increase your income - things will get easier.

It's not unusual that, despite an increase in salary, bonuses, promotions etc., you still struggle to find the money to save. In the first month following a salary increase, you often notice the additional income. However, after a while your spending also increases, because you have additional income to cover it.

Saving will only happen if you make it a priority. As the examples of Savvy Sarah shows, the important thing is for you to start saving at the earliest age possible, even if it's only a small amount. This develops a habit and it then becomes easier to consider increasing the amount you save.

The longer you leave it to start saving, the harder it becomes to start. The longer you leave it, the more ingrained the bad spending habits become.

Action Steps

Regardless of what age you are, make a commitment **today** that you will immediately start to do something to increase your wealth. If you don't take action now, you are at risk of being very poor in later life. Consider what lifestyle you are likely to have when you retire, based on your current savings habits.

If it is the lifestyle you want, then well done. Make sure you keep this up.

However, if it's a lifestyle of scrimping and struggling, then **now** is the time to do something about it.

The following chapters will look at what happens to Sarah and Nicola as they get older and continue with the habits they started in their younger years.

Chapter 2: A stitch in time

"Money is the root of all evil, and yet it is such a useful root that we cannot get on without it any more than we can without potatoes..."
- Louisa May Alcott

I'm sure you're all aware of the proverb, "a stitch in time saves nine".

Roughly translated, this means if you recognise there is a small problem, then putting effort in now to address it will prevent it from becoming a larger problem and requiring more effort to fix at a later date.

A number of you reading the previous chapter may see your spending traits mirrored in the actions of Nicola. You can compare her actions with those of Sarah and secretly wish you had the willpower, knowledge and determination to copy even a few of her savvy suggestions.

But, can you be bothered?

You enjoy spending money and live by the maxim, "You're only young once". After all, when you're older you probably won't want to go clubbing on a regular basis and spend a fortune on cocktails, will you? So, why not do it now and enjoy it while you can?

Of course, there's nothing wrong with having fun and enjoying yourself. You are only young once. However, that's the point... you only have the one opportunity to save for the time when you're no longer earning. If you don't do it whilst you're young, you may come to regret it in later years.

Let's skip forward over the next 30 years and look at what are likely to be your financial priorities at those stages in your lives. You'll also catch up with Sarah and Nicola and see how they are now getting on.

You're in your 50s

You thought childcare fees were expensive, but hadn't thought about how much it was going to cost to send both children to university. It's not like in your day when you got a grant for your living costs and certainly didn't have to pay tuition fees.

It's also an age when divorce has become very common. If it's not something you've been through yourself, chances are you know a number of couples that have experienced this. Once the children have grown up and left home, it's a sad fact that couples will often realise they don't have enough in common.

Even if the divorce has been as amicable as possible and the emotional burden is reduced, divorce will often change your financial circumstances. Household bills, which used to be covered by two people's salaries when you were married, are now only paid from one person's income when you're divorced, and living on your own.

One person living in a house does not have half the cost of two. Even if you downsize to a smaller property, all the property running costs are still very expensive and increase each year, even though your income often remains the same.

You probably ask yourself where on earth the last 25-30 years have gone. It's almost as though you blinked and you're rapidly approaching the later end of your working life.

If you started saving in your 20s, hopefully you have enough money put by. If you didn't, you may well be approaching a time when you feel you've worked for what seems like forever, but have very little savings to show for it.

If that's the case, you're probably kicking yourself that you didn't start putting some money away at a younger age, even just a small bit.

<u>Let's skip forward to see how Sarah and Nicola are getting on at this age.</u>

Savvy Sarah started saving in her 20s. She started with £25 a month, but soon found that she could increase it without it making a difference on her lifestyle. Once she started saving she could really see her cash balance increase and this spurred her on to save more.

She also got into the habit of throwing her loose change into a glass bottle at the end of each day and loved to watch the amount of coins grow. It was incredible how much that money mounted up over the course of a month. Money she didn't miss.

Sarah enjoys her job and isn't planning on retiring just yet. What she loves is that she does have enough money to retire at age 55, if she chooses. Her pension and savings won't provide a huge level of income if she retires at this age, so it wouldn't be ideal, but it's nice to know she could.

She may, in fact, choose to keep working for another 10 years. By that stage her pension and savings pot should have increased to provide her with the level of income she would like to have on a regular basis. By then, she'll be in her early 60s, so she may then retire, or at least reduce her hours.

Sarah is very grateful she started saving at such an early age. This has allowed her to have the choice of when to stop work.

Compare this to **Not-so-savvy Nicola**. Nicola didn't start saving in her 20s. In fact she didn't start saving in her 30s, either, and instead waited till she turned 40 before she set up any savings plan at all.

Even then it's only ever been a relatively small sum she's saved each month, since she's trying to get her credit card balance repaid and has a reasonably large monthly minimum payment to make on that. When she eventually has her credit card repaid that's when she plans to start to put some more money into her savings plan.

Since she's only been saving for a short period and has saved a relatively small amount, Nicola's annual pension income based on her current savings and pension plan is very low. She's aware she needs to start saving more to make a difference to her future income.

You're in your 60s

You're noticing a real "them and us" split between your friends.

Those who saved at an earlier age, or were lucky enough to have decent employer pensions, are looking forward to retiring and at last having some "me" time.

They're planning on spending more time on the golf course or tennis courts, more time with their grandchildren, and more time travelling and generally enjoying life. After all, they've worked really hard for all their working life, so now is payback time.

However, the other group of your friends would also love to have some "me" time and give up work, but can only just get by on the income they're earning. There's absolutely no chance of them having a decent lifestyle if they stop work.

Nobody wants to be part of this second group.

If you are in this latter group, whilst some of your friends are off for the day at the seaside with afternoon tea to enjoy the lovely (and rare!) beautiful English weather, you're off to work pretending you're really not jealous of them.

If you could put the clock back 30 or 40 years you would definitely have done things differently and saved more, rather than spend all your income. You did know at the back of your mind that you needed to save, but somehow you were always waiting for tomorrow.

Problem is, when you get to your 60s, tomorrow has become today... and there's not enough money in the pot.

How do Savvy Sarah and Not-so-savvy Nicola fare when they get to this age?

As you can imagine, **Savvy Sarah** is in the group of friends who go off for days out. She's joined a local tennis club, and loves to have weekends away with her friends. She will also frequently take her grandchildren out for the day and sometimes even takes them away on holiday during half term.

She does have to watch her money and has to budget. But, provided she's sensible, she feels she has enough money to do the things she enjoys. She doesn't have a particularly lavish lifestyle, but she is delighted she was a smart saver when she was earning.

Sarah chose to join her employer's pension scheme as soon as she was eligible, even though it was a contributory scheme. Since her employer matched her contribution, it made total sense for her to pay in on a monthly basis. When she became self-employed she continued with her monthly contributions. Someone had told her before that there are some tax advantages in paying into a pension. She's not fully understood what they are, but always felt that if the government were going to give her anything for free to help towards her future, she should take it.

Sarah's now absolutely delighted that she did.

Not surprisingly, **Not-so-savvy Nicola** is part of the group who grit their teeth and go off to work pretending that they don't mind the fact that they're still working many years after they had expected to retire.

She had been told, "a man is not a financial plan" but, in the absence of any other financial plan, decided she would rely on her husband to look after her financially.

Problem is, they're no longer married. In the divorce settlement Nicola opted for the house to be offset against the value of his pensions. She chose to stay in the matrimonial home to ensure her children would have the least disruption. However, she now wonders whether they should have sold the house at that stage, so she could take a smaller share of the proceeds, and have a share of the pension, too.

Nicola doesn't like to think too much about what's likely to happen in the future, since she can't see when she's likely to stop working.

You're in your 70s

The "them and us" split is even more pronounced in your 70s. One group is having great fun enjoying all the activities of the various clubs and holidays. They don't know how on earth they ever found time to work. However, the other group is still working since they can't afford to retire.

If you are in this latter group, you wonder where on earth the last 50 years have gone. You had such high hopes that you would have retired at age 50 doing just the odd bit of consultancy work to keep your hand in. However, because you haven't saved sufficiently in earlier years, you're now going to work out of necessity and can't see an end to it.

Your grandchildren have now grown up and you would have loved to spend more time with them during their childhood. However, you were working too hard and didn't have any free time.

Maybe, your grandchildren will soon have children of their own and you can offer to babysit then. Surely, you'll be able to give up work soon!

How do Savvy Sarah and Not-so-savvy Nicola fare when they get to this age?

Savvy Sarah managed to retire in her early 60s and absolutely loves her free time. Luckily, both her children were admitted to the excellent local state schools, so she and Sam didn't have to fund the huge cost of private education.

Although both children went to university, each of the kids took on part time jobs during term time and worked full time during the holidays. This meant they each made reasonable contributions towards tuition fees, accommodation and living expenses.

As a result, a significant amount of the money that Sarah and Sam had been saving for education and university costs is still intact. This has allowed them to have a reasonably comfortable retirement and enjoy more holidays than they had when they were each working.

Not-so-savvy Nicola and her husband Nathan were lucky, in that their children were also granted a place at the local state school. However, in their endeavour to keep up with the Joneses, they have spent virtually all of their working life juggling credit card balances and moving their debt from one card to another.

As soon as a new limited period interest free card is available, they pounce on it. They reason that it makes sense to take advantage of interest free, so that they can get the debt under control and repaid sooner. However, they are not using the new card sensibly and instead of using it for clever budgeting to bring their credit card balances down, they are using it instead as an excuse to spend more.

Nicola does have a small pension from work, but the monthly income is minimal, since she didn't join the scheme when she was first given the option. Although she did join many years later, her monthly contribution was low. She stopped contributing to any form of pension plan when she became self-employed.

With her many years of experience, and great reputation within her industry, she is able to do consultancy work. It's relatively lucrative when she has the business, but she's struggling to get enough enquiries to earn anywhere near the level of income she and Nathan would like.

It has only just hit them that a large house, two large cars and frequent overseas holidays are great fun and give the impression you are rolling in it. But, at some point, you need to admit to yourself that you're living beyond your means.

Why has it taken until their 70s for them to face up to it?

And, unfortunately, because Nicola has left it so late to face up to things, her financial situation only gets worse when she's in her 80s.

You're in your 80s

At last **Not-so-savvy Nicola** has stopped work. Not necessarily through choice, but her health just wasn't up to it. Money is tight, but her children help her and Nathan. She wishes it wasn't the case, but she didn't save enough to support herself, so what other option does she have?

She's pared back her expenses to a bare minimum, so she can just about get by in a normal month. However, if the car needs a service, the washing machine breaks down or birthdays or Christmas approach, there is no spare cash to cover that.

Thank goodness her children are so understanding.

What you've covered

What this chapter has shown you is that the savvy financial decisions you take during your 20s, 30s and 40s will pave the way for a more comfortable lifestyle in later years.

If you don't put the time and effort into sorting your finances at that stage you're potentially in for a difficult time as you get older.

It's very easy to stick your head in the sand and ignore your lack of financial plan. It's what a lot of women do. However, ignoring it won't make it go away. Remember, a stitch in time saves nine!

Look at the lifestyle lived by Nicola as she gets older. If this doesn't sound attractive to you (and why would it!), make a decision now to do something about it.

Action Steps

Look around at relatives, friends and colleagues who are in their 60s and older. See how much money they have and what lifestyle they are leading.

If they always appear to be short of money, ask them why they didn't save more when they were younger. The answer may be that they just didn't think about it.

If this is the case, don't end up in the same position.

Make sure you do plan now, so that you can do something to improve the amount of money you will have when you stop work. After all, nobody wants to continue to work into their 70s through necessity.

Chapter 3: Don't be an ostrich

"Money cannot buy health, but I'd settle for a diamond-studded wheelchair..." - Dorothy Parker

You all know that you should save for your future, and yet it's so easy to put it off for another day.

Initially, the reason (excuse!) is because you're very young and there's plenty of time yet. As time marches on, and more wrinkles start to appear in your complexion, you realise you're not quite as young as you thought. Yet, you still think you'll put off saving until tomorrow.

It's important to take action and plan for the future. And it's important to take action now, since the earlier you start the greater the impact on your future wealth. However, don't think that if you haven't yet done anything you shouldn't bother.

If you're worried that you've left it too late, it's all too easy to go the route of not facing up to the reality, and often decide it's better not to know.

Maybe you will fool yourselves that you have other options.

Some of the options you may have considered:

- The state
- Your husband or partner
- An inheritance
- Your children
- Hope and pray!

The state

Don't think that if you don't save for your retirement that the state will help in any significant way.

Basic state pension at the time of writing is £5,727.80 per annum (pa), which is a measly £477 per month. Anyone who thinks that's enough for them to live the life style they need, well, hats off to you! I know I certainly couldn't and most people I speak to couldn't.

Even if you don't have expensive tastes and high spending capacity, this amount has to pay all your utilities (gas, electricity, water, council tax, etc.,) and provide enough for you to eat. How much do you think will be left over after that? If you own a property you will also need to have funds to do some basic maintenance.

All that is before you've even looked at having some funds to socialise and enjoy yourself and keep yourselves clothed.

When you really stop to think about it, do you really think £477 per month will be enough?

Remember, too, that when you retire you will have more free time in your life than you've ever had before. Therefore, it's likely you will want to take up some hobbies, or spend more time doing the hobbies you didn't have enough time to enjoy whilst working.

Well, you have the time, but do you have the money? You may want to have more holidays and weekends away, because at last you have the time to enjoy your breaks.

If you've got grandchildren you may well want to treat them to some nice gifts, days out, etc.

Think about what you'd like to do when you stop working and, if you think you can achieve this on £477 per month, think again!

If you retire in your mid 60s you will probably live for another 20-30 years. The typical woman in her mid 60s these days is certainly not old. She probably doesn't even consider herself to be middle aged, yet.

She's looking forward to having time away from work to enjoy herself. However, having lots of free time doesn't sound so attractive if you can't afford to go out and do the things you want.

The government is currently discussing an increase in the basic state pension to £144 per week, which is the equivalent of £624 per month from 2016.

Although that's a reasonable increase on the current £466 per month, it's still not enough to give you a decent lifestyle. It's enough to keep you off the breadline, and that's all it was ever intended to do. But, who wants to live just above the breadline after a lifetime of hard work?

When the current style state pension was first introduced in 1948 life expectancy was significantly shorter than it is today. The pension was typically paid out for only a few years, since people did not live very long after retirement. State pension was never designed to be paid until our mid 80s and beyond.

We're all living longer and, as a result, we're placing too much burden on the state. That's why the state retirement age is increasing. For a long time, the state retirement age for women was 60. It is now gradually increasing, so that by 2018 female retirement age will be 65, in line with males.

Retirement age will then increase for both males and females to 66 from 2020, and to 67 between 2026 and 2028.

The increases in state pension age are likely to continue, as the average age of the population increases. There are less people working and contributing towards the pensions of the ever-increasing number of people who are retired and drawing pension income.

The working population pay national insurance contributions

(NIC). But, these contributions aren't going into a pot to cover your pension income when you retire. They're going into a pot that is being used to cover pension payments for people who are retired now. The government is using the contributions from those working now to pay the pensions of today's pensioners.

This means that when you retire your pension will be paid by those working at that stage. With a constantly aging population this is causing a huge financial problem for the government. Less people working are funding more and more retired people who are living for longer and longer.

It's no wonder the government needs to keep increasing the age at which they start to pay state pensions.

Many women end up relying on the state - not because it was their plan, but because they didn't plan anything else. **Do not end up in this category**. Your state pension will cover basics and keep you off the poverty line, but not a lot else.

Do you really want to have worked hard for 40 years to spend the 25 years of your retirement in poverty?

Your husband or partner

This is a common plan for women, even those who do not currently have a partner! If he's not on the scene at the minute you often assume he will magically appear at some point in the future, bearing a huge big pension pot or savings plan for you to share.

It's not a bad plan on its own. Well, not the bit about hoping he'll magically appear - the bit about relying on a real life husband's pension pot. Many couples have one pot of money, which is designed to be for the two of them when they retire.

If this is your plan, you need to check that the pension pot does in fact have enough money in it for the two of you.

So many of my female clients have told me they don't need to sort a pension because they're going to rely on their husbands' or partners' savings. Yet, when I look in detail at his pension, there's not enough there to keep one of them in a comfortable lifestyle, let alone both of them.

Many women have no idea how much money you need in your pension pot to cover the income you want each year throughout retirement. Of course, many men don't either, but this book isn't aimed at them.

An issue that is frequently ignored is that you need to consider inflation when planning your retirement income.

If you're aged in your 50s now and your latest pension statement shows a projected pension at age 65 of the amount you think you will need, you must take into account that inflation between now and aged 65 will erode the value of that pension income.

It may look a reasonable figure on the piece of paper, but by the time you get to that age it will have lost significant purchasing power due to inflation.

By looking at projected pension income in the future, and comparing that against your current income requirement as of today's date, you are not comparing like with like.

The calculation you need to do is to look at how much income you would want in today's money, and then build in an inflation factor over the years to retirement, to see what income you will need at that future date.

<u>Consider an example.</u>

Let's say you've calculated you want an annual income of £25,000 when you retire.

If you assume inflation of 3% a year, this increases to £33,598 in 10 years time, £38,950 in 15 years time, and £45,153 in 20 years time.

Your partner's pension may be showing a projected pension income of £25,000 pa at age 65, but that's not the equivalent of £25,000 in today's terms. By the time you get to retirement, that £25,000 will be worth significantly less.

If you are relying on one pension pot or savings pot to cover both of you, then for goodness sake make sure you do your sums and check it is enough for both of you. Remember, your partner may not have a clue about finance, either! He may well think he has and think he's got it all under control, but ask him to go through the calculations with you.

Work out what income you need when you retire, calculate what that will be after adding inflation and compare that to the projected income from the pension plan.

If that previous sentence left you in a cold sweat, call in an adviser to help you with the calculation.

The sooner you work out whether you have enough money when you retire, the easier it will be to take action to correct the situation if the figure isn't enough. Sticking your head in the sand and ignoring the issue is never a sensible option. It's much better to find out exactly what the position is and what you can do to improve things.

Divorce

We haven't even mentioned the "D" word yet. Divorce statistics are scary, since currently 42% of marriages in the UK end in divorce. This is too big a number to ignore the impact of getting divorced on your finances.

Of course, if you're currently happily married, or in a civil partnership, you don't want to spend too much time considering what would happen to you if your relationship were to fail. The fact is, that as well as causing extreme emotional upset, it could significantly mess up your finances.

In the following I have used the term "husband" for ease of reading to avoid at each stage having to write "husband/spouse/partner". However, the comments made in regard to a husband also apply to a civil/married partner in a same sex relationship if you had been through a legal ceremony.

Your husband's pension will be taken into account in the financial settlement. But, you will now run two houses, rather than one. You are, therefore, bound to be in a worse state financially than when you were married. The same amount of income is coming in, but it is now covering additional expenses.

If you have young children you may choose to stay in the marital home to avoid too much disruption for the children. However, if you end up with sole ownership of the marital home after the divorce settlement, then it's likely your husband will end up with his entire pension intact as a trade off.

You have a large sized home and at some point you plan to downsize. However, depending on where you live, downsizing may not release much equity. You'll probably still want a reasonable sized home, so children and grandchildren can come to stay.

Don't assume that downsizing is an option that will provide sufficient funds for your retirement. It may release some capital, but is it likely to be enough to fund your retirement needs?

If you have been a stay at home mum during your marriage, looking after the children and the home, you need to know there's a double whammy regarding state pension, which impacts mainly on women.

To receive the full state pension you need to have worked and paid NIC for a minimum of 35 years. You do, however, get credit for periods you were not working when you were at home bringing up children under the age of 12.

However, depending on your work history, if you've been a stay at home mother you may not have accrued your 35 years worth of NIC. For each year under 35, the state pension is reduced accordingly.

Currently, following divorce, one partner's NIC record can be substituted from one party to the other. As an example, if a wife had not accrued sufficient NIC during her lifetime to qualify for the minimum basic state pension, she could rely on her husband's record to become eligible for the payment. The Department of Work and Pensions (DWP) will substitute the ex-husband's NIC record for hers at no cost to either party.

From April 2016, following the introduction of the new state pension, this will no longer be possible.

Relying on your husband's pension is an option used by many women. However, it comes with a health warning. Do check your individual circumstances and see that it's an appropriate plan for you.

Again, the comments above would also apply to a civil/married partner in a same sex relationship if you've been through a legal ceremony.

However, it <u>doesn't</u> apply to a relationship where you're living with your partner and not married, or not in a legal civil partnership. Although many people refer to "common-law- wife", it's a myth, and has no legal standing whatsoever.

If you are living with your partner and not married there are no laws that say your partner's pension must be shared with you if you separate. This is the situation even if you have been living together for many years and have children together. If you're living in your partner's house and your name is not on the deeds, don't assume that if you separate the courts will automatically give you a share.

If you are in this situation seek legal advice urgently and consider preparing a co-habitation agreement to protect yourself in a worst-case scenario.

An inheritance

Depending on your age, it wouldn't be unusual for your parents to have bought a house for a tiny sum that is now worth a small fortune, due to the large increases in house values over the years.

Whilst I'm sure you're not planning the demise of either parent, it may well have occurred to you that there's a future inheritance available to fund your retirement.

However a few things to bear in mind:

You have no idea at what age you will receive your inheritance. Your parents could live to their mid 90s and beyond. Depending on how old they were when you were born, you could be well past your planned retirement age at this stage.

Consider, also, that inheritance tax kicks in at 40% on the value of any estate over £325,000, and this will reduce your inheritance significantly.

Another issue to consider is that, in the future, your parents may need long term care. We are all living much longer than earlier generations, but we are not necessarily as healthy as we'd like to be in later years. If your parents need long term care, the value of their estate may be used to pay for it.

Relying on an inheritance is a very poor plan.

Not only do you have no control over when you can access the funds, you also have no idea what funds will be available. Long term care costs and inheritance tax could significantly erode the value of your inheritance.

When your inheritance eventually does arrive, it may be nowhere near the amount you had anticipated when you initially considered this to be your ideal financial plan.

Your children

Your plan may be that when you're ready to retire and funds are low, then it's payback time for your children.

You've looked after them for years, and scrimped and saved so that they could have all the things they wanted. As a result, you had no money left to save anything for your own future. So, now you plan to go to them and ask them to help out.

Whilst many children would be very willing to help their parents, you do have to consider the state of their finances. Depending on their age, they may be saddled with an enormous mortgage and may, themselves, be struggling to find sufficient funds to cover their outgoings. There won't necessarily be anything in the pot to help you.

This is a very dangerous plan. Much better to have your own plan and then, if your children can help out, that's an added bonus.

Hope and pray

As a financial planner, I'm never going to advocate that this is a sensible plan. Hope is not a strategy.

If you have this as your plan and realise when you get there that this hasn't worked - in fact, the universe didn't provide - it's then too late to do anything about it.

Much better to have a separate plan and then, if the universe somehow gives you all you need when you retire, you're going to be feeling very comfortable indeed. You'll have more than enough and will really be able to enjoy your retirement years in abundance.

Don't you think this is a much better plan than the alternative?

So what now?

We've looked at a number of different plans and strategies for having income when you retire. The one strategy we haven't yet looked at is **taking action and sorting it for yourself**.

The Spice Girls had it right with the term, "girl power". Or maybe you prefer the adage, "If you want a job done properly, do it yourself".

Whether or not you were a fan of The Spice Girls, take a leaf out of their book and take action to sort your future yourself. Why? Because, as L'Oreal says, "You're worth it".

What you've covered

There are several options available to fool yourself you will have a comfortable lifestyle when you retire. These options range from sticking your head in the sand and ignoring the whole issue, to relying on others to sort the problem for you.

Apart from the option of sharing your husband's or partner's pension, which **may** be a sensible option depending on the circumstances, the rest are riddled with problems and are not good suggestions at all.

The only sensible plan to have is to take responsibility yourself and take whatever action is necessary to save sufficient funds.

Action Steps

Be honest with yourself and look at what plan you have for income when you stop work. If your head is in the sand, then get it out of there! The sooner you face up to the fact you don't have a sensible plan in place, the easier it will be to get a plan together and move forwards.

Be brave. Stand up now and say, "My name's Mary Waring (obviously insert your own name here!), and I admit I don't have a financial plan."

Doesn't that make you feel better?

The following chapters will show you what you can do to put your plan in place.

Chapter 4: And we're off

"People say money is not the key to happiness, but I always figured if you have enough money, you can have a key made..." - *Joan Rivers*

Congratulations, you've started on your journey to improving your finances! Maybe, you were determined when you first bought the book to get your finances under control once and for all, or it might be that I frightened the life out of you in the previous chapters. Maybe, I left you in such a cold sweat you felt you just had to keep reading.

Either way, well done. It's now time to get down to the nitty gritty.

In order to be in the position where you can set a goal for your wealth and measure your improvements you obviously need to begin by knowing your starting point. Otherwise, you've got no way of knowing whether you've improved your position or how much the improvement is.

Calculate your net worth

The starting point is to calculate your "net worth".

A basic spreadsheet has been included at http://www.mary-waring. co.uk/TheWW-networth/. Use this as a template and adjust it to meet your personal circumstances. Complete the boxes in yellow. The spreadsheet has formulas to calculate total assets, total liabilities and net worth.

A copy of the spreadsheet is shown in Appendix I. Since you will be updating this on a regular basis it would be best to photocopy this sheet to complete it rather than write in the book.

Alternatively start from a blank sheet of paper and draw a line down the middle of it. Label up the left hand column "Assets".

Your assets represent everything you own.

The items that will go in this column:

- Your house, if you own it. At this stage ignore any mortgage you may have on the house and simply write down its value
- Any investment property you own - either a holiday cottage or buy to let
- Your car
- Investments - ISAs, unit trusts, stocks and shares, etc
- Savings pots
- Money in the bank
- Premium bonds
- Pensions
- Endowments
- Cash

You'll need to do a bit of research, first, to find the value of everything. Contact all your pension and savings providers and request an up to date statement. Once you have the values noted down, add them all up to get a total value of everything you own.

This represents your total assets

If you have antique furniture, or some furniture of high values, then include these in the calculation. Certainly don't bother with adding up the value of tables, chairs and your general household furniture. It's just not worth the effort.

If you have valuable jewellery, then do include that in your calculations. Don't bother including all the jewellery you own unless it's of decent value.

You need to be able to repeat this exercise on a regular basis, so the easier you can make the whole process the better. To help with this,

I suggest you use an electronic spreadsheet, so that you always have a template of what you've included and then all you need to do is just update the values.

Having calculated your total assets, move over to the right hand column and head this up "Liabilities".

<u>Liabilities represent everything you owe.</u>

The items to be included in this column:

- The outstanding value of any mortgages - either on your main residence, or on an investment property
- Any amounts owed on hire purchase, or loan agreements
- Amounts outstanding on your credit cards
- Student loans
- Overdraft
- Amounts owed to family or friends

Once you have all the figures, add this up to get your **total liabilities**.

Net worth is calculated as your total assets, less your total liabilities.

This has now given you a starting point and will be your base calculation.

What you now need to do is to set yourself a goal for what you would like your net worth to be in, say, six months time, or a year's time. You can either set a specific monetary figure, or you can aim to increase your current net worth by a certain percentage.

The goal you set will depend on your starting point and your own specific circumstances.

For example, if your net worth is £50,000 today and you earn an average income, it would be pointless to set a target of achieving a net worth of £300,000 in a year's time. You would be setting yourself up for failure, which would make it very likely you would then give up at an early stage.

Similarly, if your net worth is £500,000 now and you earn a very decent income, you'd probably want to set yourself a goal higher than growing your wealth to £501,000 in a year's time.

Take some time to do this exercise by considering what income and spending you have each month, and what amount you believe you could save on a regular basis.

There has to be some science behind your figure, rather than plucking any number that sounds about right. More detail on how to look at your income and spending will be provided in Chapter 7 "In out, in out, shake it all about".

SMART goal setting

Like all goal setting you want to follow the SMART approach.

S = Specific: your goal must be specific, rather than general. Instead of having a goal "I want to increase my wealth", you should have a goal "I want to increase my wealth by £x", or "I want to increase my wealth by x% more than it is today"

If your current net worth is £100,000 then a goal of "I want to increase my wealth" would be met if your wealth increased to £100,001", but that may not be what you want.

The more specific you can be, the better. This will help with your planning.

M = measurable: your goal must be capable of being measured against concrete criteria. If you set a specific goal, as in the example above, then you know it will be measurable. You recalculate your net worth at whatever interval you have chosen (e.g., six months or one year) and then see whether you are on target.

A = Attainable: your goal must be realistic and attainable. It should stretch you, but not be so extreme that it cannot be achieved. In the example used above, if someone with a net worth of £50,000 today earning an average salary set a goal to achieve a net worth of £300,000 in a year's time, I suggest this would be neither realistic nor attainable.

Similarly for someone with a net worth of £500,000 now earning a very decent income, a goal of growing their net worth to £501,000 would not stretch them sufficiently. Chances are they could achieve this without trying very hard.

Your goal should stretch you. Make it a "knee trembling" goal. However, you do need to believe that it is achievable provided you put in great effort. If you don't believe it's achievable, you may not try hard enough to reach it.

R = Relevant: your goal must drive you forward. For example, you may want to improve your financial position, so that you are able to retire at an earlier age, or be able to send your children to private school. Choose whatever your greatest motivator is and use this when you need a little bit of extra drive to move you towards your goal. The more you can imagine you have attained your goal and are enjoying the life you'll lead when you get there, the more you will want to strive to achieve it.

Spend some time each day imagining that you have achieved your goal. What will your typical day be like once you're successful? What do you see, hear, feel and say? The more real you can make the experience, the more it will spur you on to attain it.

Prepare a mood board of what life will be like, and fill it with glorious pictures and images that represent your ideal life when your goal has been achieved. Have the board hanging in a spot where you will view it each day, so that your subconscious has the opportunity to really experience the life you are planning.

T = Time-bound: your goal must have a timescale attached to it. Instead of having a goal "I want to increase my net worth in the future", set a goal "I want to have increased my net worth to £x by 31.12.20xx", for example. Then, when you have reached this date and measured your progress, set the next goal for another six months or 12 months ahead.

Check regularly

Repeat the net worth exercise on a regular basis to check whether you are on track to reach the goals you have set. If you're not on track, instead of getting despondent and thinking the exercise has failed, consider whether your goal was set correctly.

It's very easy when fired up with enthusiasm to set a goal, which looks reasonable at day one, but has not taken into account the few little hiccups that may happen along the way - the major car maintenance bill, or the three weddings this year you hadn't included in your budget.

Build some slack into your calculations, so that when unplanned expenditure comes along you are able to fit it into your budget, without going off course.

If you haven't met your goal when you carry out your review exercise, instead of being fed up you haven't reached the goal, think about what you can learn from the process. If your goal was too ambitious, then recognise this and use this information when you set your target for the next period. Consider now whether your increase in wealth has, in fact, been a great success, even if you haven't met the goal you'd previously set.

An increase in wealth from £50,000 to £55,000 over the year should be still be acknowledged and celebrated, even if your target was to reach £60,000.

If you didn't achieve your goal, but in fact you've now decided your goal was set too high, consider with hindsight what goal you would have set.

If the reason why your goal hasn't been achieved is because you didn't follow the principles of improving your wealth as well as you should, then use this as a learning tool for the next period.

Recognise that setting a goal at day one will only be as accurate as the effort you put in to achieve it. If it's a half-hearted effort, then it's highly unlikely the goal will be met.

If, up to now, you've had a number of years of over-spending with no pattern of regular saving, then it will take a time to get new habits in place. Recognise this, and try not to be too despondent if you haven't reached your target.

I said earlier that this book is not a get rich quick scheme. It's a process to follow to improve your wealth over time. Sometimes, you will follow the process to the letter and see a significant improvement in your finances. At other times, it may be harder and maybe you won't move forward at all.

Recognise that it is the small steps you take on a regular basis that will lead to good results over the long term. If you have a period of non-achievement, or a period during which you don't move forward as well as you had hoped, put that down to learning experience. Then start again with renewed vigour.

This is a long term project. If you have a few hiccups along the way, learn from them and move on. It's the results you achieve over the long term that will be the deciding factor on your wealth, rather than what you achieve over a short period.

What if your net worth is more than you had planned?

Remember, when you do your first measurement you may be ahead of plan, rather than behind it. Again, consider what you can learn from this. Maybe, you were so enthused to start with that you put 100% effort into growing your wealth and overshot your goal.

If you are unlikely to be able to keep up this level of effort on a long term basis, then chances are you won't do such a sterling job over the next period. Keep this in mind when setting your next short term goal.

Alternatively, perhaps you were just ultra cautious in your plans. If so, bear this in mind when you set your target for the next period.

The whole measurement process is designed to show you how sensible your goals were and how far you have progressed towards achieving them.

Feedback on both areas can then be used to determine what your goals should be for the next stage. Learn what you can from the experience and then use this feedback to determine your goals for the next period.

What if your net worth is negative?

If your net worth is negative it means that you owe more than you own. It's not a great starting point. If you're in that position you probably had a sneaking feeling that was the case, and maybe you stuck your head in the sand ignoring it.

If you are in this position, at least once you know about it you can start to take steps to correct the situation.

You need to get to a positive net worth position as soon as possible. Make this an absolute priority. Instead of getting worried about your starting point, and maybe allowing that fear and worry to stop you doing anything about it, concentrate at this stage on how you can reduce the negative figure.

Let this be the incentive you need to keep you going.

How do you increase your net worth?

We've said above that net worth is:

Total assets, less total liabilities.

Therefore, from a pure mathematical point of view, the way to increase your net worth is either:

a)   Increase your assets (what you own) or
b)   Reduce your liabilities (what you owe)

In an ideal world you'd do both at the same time in order to see greater improvement.

In the following chapters we will look at each of the above options to show how you can achieve this.

What you've covered

In order to set a goal for improving your wealth you need to calculate your starting point, which is represented by your net worth. This is calculated as your total assets (what you own), less your total liabilities (what you owe).

Having calculated a starting point you then need to set a target for what you want this figure to be in six months or 12 months.

This then becomes an ongoing process of calculating your net worth figure at regular intervals, comparing to the target and then setting your goal for the next period.

Action Steps

Set up an electronic spreadsheet and list all your assets (what you own) in the left hand column and your liabilities (what you owe) in the right hand column. Fill in all figures now, even if it's very rough. Use Appendix I or the spreadsheet on my website as an example.

You can get more accurate figures at a later date, but for now use whatever are the most recent figures you can get hold of.

Then consider, what do you want the figures to be in six months or 12 months? Write this figure down.

Chapter 5: Till debt us do part

"Money will not buy happiness, but I'd rather cry in a Jaguar than on a bus..." - Françoise Sagon

Research from Credit Action (a financial charity) shows that the average debt excluding mortgage for an adult in the UK is £3,190. That may not sound a huge amount, but let's have a think about exactly what that means.

The average salary in the UK is circa £25,000 pa. After tax and national insurance, that will net down to roughly £18,500 take home pay each year, which is about £1,500 per month. A debt of £3,190 therefore represents over two months' worth of take home pay.

In other words, if you didn't need any of your salary to live on and you could use all of your monthly income to repay your debts, it would take more than two months to get the debt fully paid off.

Since it's totally impractical to suggest you could use all of your salary to pay off your debt, how long would it take to get this debt repaid if you were earning an average salary and using a more practical approach?

If you work on a figure of using 20% of your take home pay to repay the debt, it would take over a year to get it fully paid back - and that of course assumes you are not adding to the debt at any point during that period.

The figures for some individuals are, much worse than this, because, as with all averages, some people will be well below average and some above. Since a number of people will have no debt, this means that for each individual who repays their credit card bill in full each month, another individual will have double the average - over £6,500 in credit card debt.

How long would it take to repay your debt?

If you're running up debt balances, do a very rough calculation straight away as to how long it would take to repay your current balance.

Firstly, work out what income you typically have after tax and national insurance each month. If you're employed, that's quite easy. Either take the net salary on your last pay slip, or use the annual figures in your most recent P60, and divide by 12.

If you're self-employed, this may be slightly more difficult, since potentially your income varies from month to month. Some months you may have great success in your business and have high income. However, there may also be months with much lower income.

One way to estimate this is to look at your last tax return to see your net earnings (after tax and national insurance) for the last tax year. If you believe that, during this current tax year, your income will either increase or decrease from last year's figure, then make an estimate of what the figure is likely to be now. Again, divide this figure by 12 to get a monthly figure.

There's a certain amount of guess work and estimation involved, but it doesn't matter, since it's only a very theoretical exercise. It's not practical to suggest you can use all your income over any period of time to pay off your debt, without needing any of that income to live on. You are simply using this calculation as a starting point.

Secondly, calculate how many months worth of net income your debt represents. In this exercise your debt should include credit cards, car finance, retail finances, overdraft and unsecured loans.

Whatever the number of months you've just calculated, multiply that number by six. This will represent very roughly how many months it would take to repay the debt if you used 20% of your net income each month to bring the debt down.

The process can be summarised as follows:

Step 1: calculate your net take home pay per month.

Step 2: total all your outstanding debt balances, excluding your mortgage balance.

Step 3: divide the total figure calculated in step 2, by the figure calculate in step 1. This calculates how many months worth of your take home pay your debt represents. In other words, if you didn't need to use your take home pay for anything else other than repaying your debt, this is how many months it would take to repay the debt.

Step 4: Multiply the figure calculated in step 3 by six, to estimate how many months it would take to repay the total debt if your debt repayments were 20% of your monthly take home pay.

Example

Step 1: Let's assume you earn £25,000 per annum, which, as shown above, represents circa £1,500 take home pay per month.

Step 2: Let's assume your credit card, overdraft and car loan balances totalled £6,000.

Step 3: £6,000 divided by £1,500 is four. This means that your debt represents four months' worth of your take home pay.

Step 4: The four months calculated in step 3 is multiplied by six to give 24 months i.e., two years.

What this example has calculated is that, if you earn £25,000 pa and have debt balances of £6,000, it will take you 24 months (two years) to get the debt fully repaid if you use 20% of your take home pay each month to repay the debts.

Using take home pay of £1,500 as an example, the amount you will repay on your debt each month will be £300 i.e., 20% of £1,500.

Remember, of course, this example assumes no new debt is being added during the 24 months period. The example assumes credit card and other debt balances are only reducing during this period and not increasing.

This is a rough calculation and the actual number of months will vary depending on exactly what interest rate you are charged on the debts. However, it is a useful starting point to give a guide as to how long it would take you the repay your debts, based on the assumption of using 20% of your take home pay for repayments each month.

Can you afford to pay back 20% of your net income?

Consider how practical it is that you could spend as much as 20% of your take home pay each month repaying your debt.

A number of reports suggest that, a rule of thumb for how large a mortgage you could afford to repay, is that your monthly mortgage repayments should be no more than about 25%-30% of your monthly net income.

The above calculation has, therefore, assumed that you are repaying a similar amount on your credit card and other unsecured debt, as you are repaying on your mortgage.

Does that fit in with your budget?

If not, and you are repaying much less than 20%, then the period of time it will take to repay your debts is obviously significantly longer.

How much longer depends on how much less than the 20% you repay each month.

Don't assume that if you repay 10%, rather than 20%, that you simply double the number of months. For example, using the figures in the example above, if you reduced your debts by 10% of your take home pay each month, rather than 20%, the number of months to get the debt fully repaid would increase from 24 months to about 56 months.

Why is it more than double the 24 months?

This is because your debt keeps clocking up interest for as long as it is outstanding. The longer it takes to repay your debt, the more interest you will be charged. Therefore, in the example above, repaying 10% of your take home pay, rather than 20%, has increased the time it takes to repay the debt and also increased the interest charged.

If you do have outstanding debt, then doing this calculation may be enough of a wake up call for you to do something about it. If so, great. We'll be coming on to exactly what you can do about it in a minute.

We live in an "instant gratification" society. If you want to buy something, chances are you want it NOW, regardless of whether you can afford it or not. In a number of instances that's not such a big problem. You buy your big purchase now and pay it off over the next couple of months.

However, it becomes much more of an issue if you keep doing this month in, month out, and you have no plan as to how you are going to get your credit card balances repaid. If this sounds familiar to you, the good news is that you are in great company. There are loads and loads of people in the UK doing exactly the same thing.

Then again, the bad news is this is certainly one instance where you don't want to be part of the crowd.

Wake up and smell the coffee

At some point you have to wake up to the fact you are overspending and cannot continue doing this. If you are spending on your credit card each month and unable to pay it back at the end of the month, the figures can very easily get out of control.

Maybe you're kidding yourself you can stay on top of it. Maybe, you're expecting a bonus or a pay rise next year. Perhaps you're self-employed and you have great plans for your business next year, which should significantly increase your income.

Here's a very radical thought! Why not wait until you've earned that bonus, salary rise, or extra income before you spend it? After all, that's exactly what your parents and grandparents did in earlier generations when credit was not so readily available. They thought about what they wanted and then saved up until they could afford to buy it.

How many of you have gone out and bought something on the spur of the moment, on a credit card, without stopping to think for any period of time whether it's something you really want? In many cases, when you get home it's not so great at all.

Sometimes, you take it back to the shop and get a refund, but sometimes it just sits in the wardrobe gathering dust and eventually ends up at the charity shop.

The wardrobe may be full of clothes, but you can still say, "I've got nothing to wear."

Shopping during a sale is the time when this is very likely to happen. You get so caught up in being pleased with yourself that you've nabbed a real bargain that you forget the fact that what you've just spent your hard earned money on is not really something you wanted at all.

Far from being a real bargain, the "3 for 2" offer sounded great until you consider that you actually only wanted one item. Far from getting a bargain by receiving one item free, you've actually paid for one item that you didn't even need or want.

<u>Facts and figures about debt</u>

Let me show you some facts and figures about debt and how long it can take to get a debt balance repaid. I'm going to use the example of a credit card, but in fact the same principle applies for all forms of debt.

Firstly, consider the interest rate you are paying on your credit card.

Despite the fact that at the time of writing the Bank of England base rate is 0.5%, interest on your credit card will be in the region of 17%. If it's a store card, the rate will be circa 23%, or more.

So, the first thing to do is to find out exactly what rate you are paying on your credit card. It's not always that obvious from your statements, so you may need to phone the credit card provider to find out. Your statement is likely to show you something along the lines of 1.3% per month.

This sounds a nice low figure because it begins with a "1". However, bear in mind that if you don't pay your balance off in full this month, the part that is unpaid will have 1.3% interest added to it next month. The following month it has 1.3% interest added again. But in addition, you will also pay 1.3% interest on the interest you were charged in month one.

This is known as compounding.

It means that an interest of 1.3% per month actually compounds to circa 17% interest per annum. It's not just a case of taking the monthly figure and then multiplying by 12. The actual answer is more than this, since you are paying interest on interest.

For many people, finding out just how expensive your credit card really is, and realising exactly how much profit the credit card company is making from you and your impulse purchases, may be enough to put a bit of a rein on your spending.

If you haven't really thought about it before, it's easy to be in denial. However, I suggest you phone your credit card provider and find out exactly how much you are paying and see if that impacts on your desire to keep using your flexible friend.

Make sure you ask them to tell you the annual percentage rate - not the monthly one. It's the annual percentage rate that is likely to send shivers down your spine. Therefore, if you want to reduce your credit card spending, this is the figure you need to know.

You also need to be aware of how credit card companies calculate the amount you repay each month. It will typically be 2% of the outstanding balance, subject to a minimum payment of £5.

Therefore, in a scenario where you have a balance on your credit card that you are paying down each month, the minimum payment will also reduce each month as your outstanding debt balance reduces.

For example, suppose you have a balance of £5,000 on your card at day one. Initially, 2% of this is £100. So your minimum payment will be £100 per month at the start. At a future date, when the balance has reduced to say, £4,000, the minimum payment will be reduced to £80 per month (being 2% of £4,000).

Credit card companies aren't doing this to be kind to you, or because they want you to have an easier time repaying the balance. They do it because they earn a HUGE amount of interest by doing so.

From their point of view, the longer it takes you to repay the balance on your card, the better. This is because they will continue to charge you interest each month, and then the following month charge you interest on the interest.

To see what effect this has in practise, let's look at an example. First, a word of warning:

If you haven't seen this type of example before, I warn you now you're in for a shock.

Balance outstanding	£5,000
Minimum payment	2% of the outstanding balance each month, subject to a minimum payment of £5
Interest rate	17%.

In this example I'm going to assume you're not going to add anything to the credit card balance, since you're just aiming to get the balance paid off over time.

Have a think about how long you think it would take for the balance to be repaid if you only paid the minimum balance each month. Remember that, as your debt reduces, your monthly payment will also reduce.

You may have thought somewhere around seven years. Maybe, you thought you'd go for the highest guess you thought it could be and went for somewhere nearer 20 years.

If so, then be prepared for a shock, because the actual number is 47 years. Yes, just in case you thought that was a typo, I'm going to say it again; it's **47 years**.

If the example is similar to your own situation, this means that, unless you're aged about 20, you will still be paying off the balance when you retire.

You'd certainly still be paying for it long after the item you purchased has gone out of fashion (and come in and gone out again a few times!), and long after it's become obsolete, broken, or ended up in the charity shop.

Who wants to buy something on a credit card that will take 47 years to repay?

The other horror to consider is how much you will have repaid over the 47 year period.

In the example above, you'll actually have repaid £15,750. Bearing in mind the initial purchase was for £5,000, by putting it on credit card and repaying only the minimum balance each month, you've repaid over three times the initial cost.

Once you know this, the question to ask yourself each time you're considering putting a purchase on a credit card and repaying over time is, *"Do I still want this if it's going to cost about three times that amount"?*

The holiday you'd love to go on that costs £1,000 may not look so attractive if the cost is going to be over £3,000, by the time you've repaid it.

It's too easy to look at a purchase and think, "it's only going to cost me £20 a month to pay that off" and consider that a bargain. However, before you go ahead and purchase, work out how much it's costing you in total, and then consider whether you still want to purchase it.

How do you improve the position?

Of course, what the credit card companies don't tell you is that there are a few easy ways to improve this position.

Let's look back at the previous example of £5,000 outstanding on your credit card, where you started to repay £100 per month. What if, instead of reducing this monthly repayment as your balance reduced, you actually kept your monthly repayment at £100?

It's very easy to consider that if the credit card company is only asking for £80, you may as well only pay them £80. But, now that you know the impact of this, you may think differently.

If you recalculate the figures on the basis that you will continue to repay a constant £100 each month, the figures may surprise you.

In this case, the period of time it takes you to repay your debt is seven years - a wonderful reduction on the initial 47 year period. Over those seven years the total cost will be £8,476.

Compared to £15,750 in the first example, the total amount repaid has reduced by almost half.

Of course, the interesting thing is that it doesn't involve finding any extra money.

You've simply not reduced the monthly repayment, as your debt has reduced.

If you could afford to repay £100 in month one, there's no reason why you can't afford to repay this amount in each of the following months. It's simply that you agree to pay the lower amount when the credit card company asks for a lower minimum payment.

Let's take this a stage further and assume that, having calculated all these figures, you decide you want to get the debt repaid as quickly as possible. You're willing to pay back £200 at the beginning of the period and keep repaying this figure constantly each month.

This will then reduce the repayment period to two and a half years with a total repayment figure of £6,099. Since the initial loan was for £5,000, your interest in this example is £1,099. Compared to an interest cost in excess of £10,000 in the first example, this is a massive saving.

Here's a summary of the above figures:

Monthly payment	Years to repay balance	Amount repaid
£100 reducing	47 years	£15,750
£100 level	7 years	£8,476
£200 level	2½ years	£6,099

The main principle to take from this is that the smaller the amount you repay each month, the longer the period it will take for you to get the balance repaid. The longer it takes to get the balance repaid, the greater the interest cost.

This principle applies to all forms of loans and debt. If you're arranging a personal loan, or a loan for a car purchase, always consider what you will repay in total, not just what you repay each month. To reduce the total amount repayable, consider whether you should take the loan over five years, rather than seven years.

Ask the finance company to provide quotes over a number of different time periods, so that you can compare them and see the effect of paying a smaller amount each month.

What about a mortgage?

This same approach should be applied when you are discussing your mortgage. Don't automatically arrange a mortgage that takes you to your planned retirement age. Think in advance about what amount you can afford to pay each month, and then, maybe, consider having a 20 year mortgage rather than 25 years.

Ask the lender for an illustration for both options and see how much extra interest you will pay with the longer period option.

Always make sure you when you remortgage that you do so for the period of time left on your existing mortgage - or a lower period if possible. Don't keep remortgaging for 20 years each time because you like the fact this reduces your monthly repayment.

It looks attractive at the time to pay a lower amount each month, but this will have a huge impact on how much you pay in total.

Now that you know this, you will be able to ask for a number of illustrations over different time periods and compare.

Cash or credit?

I have seen research which shows that if you use a credit card when you go shopping, you are likely to spend 212% of the amount you would have spent if you were to pay by cash. In other words, you will spend twice as much by using a credit card. I'm sure you can all relate to this.

How many times have you gone shopping and purchased something with a credit card that you wouldn't have bought if you had to pay by cash?

The same research has shown that, even if you pay your balance off in full each month, you will still overspend by 30% (almost one third) by using a credit card, rather than cash.

This means that for each £100 you would spend if you were paying for your purchases by cash, you will spend £130 if you were paying with a by credit card - even when you repay the card balance in full at the end of each month.

If you don't repay the balance in full each month, you'll probably spend £212 on your credit card, instead of the £100 you'll spend if you were paying cash.

To find out whether this is true for you, why not try it out? For a certain period of time, only pay for things by cash or debit card. This provides an automatic stop on your spending, because if you don't have an overdraft facility (and if you do, don't use it during this trial period) you have to stop spending when you don't have any money left in your account.

How about trying it for a month to see what impact this has on your spending patterns? You may prefer to keep this habit on a permanent basis going forwards. You never know, it could be the biggest positive impact on improving your wealth, without you feeling that you've given up spending on things that you enjoy.

Credit cards are great, and we do all need them. There will always be the big bill for which you haven't budgeted. Maybe your car breaks down unexpectedly, or perhaps the roof has a leak. There will always be times when you would be in a very difficult position without a credit card, but they have to be used carefully.

Don't allow yourself to be the person that the credit card companies can't wait to get their hands on because you're such a great profit earner for them.

Use them wisely so that they are working for you, not working for the credit card company.

What you've covered

The important thing to consider with credit is not how much you are paying back each month, but how much you are paying back in total.

The less you pay each month, the longer it will take to get the debt repaid, and the more it will cost.

In the credit card example, paying back only the minimum each month took 47 years to get the debt repaid and cost over three times the original purchase cost. However, continuing

---

to repay the same amount each month - and not reduce it as the debt reduces - resulted in a saving of around half the amount, and took seven years to repay.

This is an incredible saving, considering that did not involve finding any extra money. It simply relied on not reducing the payment as the debt reduced.

Action steps

Find out what interest rate you are paying on your credit card. If you are running an ongoing balance, which you are paying off over time, see if there are better offers available. Although there are cards with 0% interest for a limited period of time, a number of these now charge a fee to transfer a balance from another card. Do take this into account in all your calculations.

Aim to repay your debts as quickly as possible. Always look at what you're paying in total, rather than just consider the monthly repayment amount.

For a period of time, try spending just using a debit card, or cash, and see what impact this has on your spending. Has it significantly reduced your spending, without you even realising?

Chapter 6: Getting interesting

"It's not the creation of wealth that is wrong, but the love of money for its own sake..." - Margaret Thatcher

In the previous chapter, you saw the horror of how compound interest works against you when you owe money. Being charged interest on interest seriously adds to debt.

What you need to do, therefore, is find a way to make compounding work in your favour.

If interest on interest makes your debt increase when you owe money, do you think it's possible that it can make your savings increase in the same way when you have money on deposit, rather than owe it? Of course it can.

Let's look at a quick example.

Assume you have just paid £1,000 into your bank deposit account and you're getting 10% interest per year on it. I absolutely accept that you won't get 10% interest in the bank based on today's interest rates, but using 10% as the figure makes the numbers easier to follow. Also, at this stage I want to concentrate on the principle of compounding, rather than get bogged down with specific figures.

If you had £1,000 on deposit at day one, at the end of the first year you will earn 10% interest on the £1,000, i.e., £100. If you were to leave the interest you've earned in the bank rather than withdraw it, you now have £1,100 as your bank balance.

At the end of year two you get 10% interest on the initial £1,000 as before - i.e., £100. However, you also get 10% interest on the

£100 interest earned in year one, i.e., £10. Total interest at the end of year two is £110. Again, assuming you keep this interest in the bank rather than withdraw it, you now have a total bank balance of £1,210.

At the end of year three, you get 10% interest on the initial £1,000 (£100), 10% interest on the £100 interest earned in year one (i.e., £10) and 10% interest on the £10 interest earned in year two (i.e., £1). Total interest earned during year three is £111, and the total balance now is £1,321.

In table form it will look like:

Invest	Year 1 £	Year 2 £	Year 3 £
£1,000	100	100	100
£100		10	10
£10			1
£1			
Balance at end of year	£1,100	£1,210	£1,321

If you continued this exercise for 10 years, at the end of year 10 the £1,000 initially deposited would now be worth £2,594. Since no additional capital was added to the bank account after the initial £1,000 deposit, the growth has come purely from interest and, more specifically, the effect of compounding interest, i.e., interest on interest. Over the 10 year period, interest on the £1,000 on its own would have been £1,000. This means that an additional £594 has come from the compounding principle. This represents over one third of the total interest received.

"The Slight Edge"

I want to share with you an example from "The Slight Edge" by Jeff Olson, published by Success Books, 2011. The principle of the book is how small changes carried out consistently over a long period of time can have a significant impact. Each action, on its own, is very small and will not result in much of an effect immediately. For that reason, although it's very easy to do the small action, it's also very easy to not bother to take action.

The positive effect of taking the action is minimal, but the negative effect of not taking the action is also minimal. As a result, that makes it very easy not to do it, since there is no significant downside at that time if you don't take action.

Jeff Olson gives a wonderful example of the principle at work.

He tells the story of a wealthy man who is about to die and who will bequeath his significant wealth to his twin sons. He gives each of them a choice: either accept £1 million now, as a one-off sum, or accept 1p now, with the condition that the balance in the bank account will be doubled each day for the following 31 days. At the end of the 31 days the son with the most money inherits the rest of his fortune. (The tale is originally told in dollars and cents, but I have adjusted it to British currency.)

Son 1 takes the £1 million and hires a team of advisers to help him manage his fortune.

Son 2 takes 1p. On day two he is then given another penny to make his balance 2p. At the end of day three he is given another 2p to bring his balance up to 4p.

Half way through week three the two sons meet up. Son 1 is investing his £1 million and planning what to spend it on. Son 2, at this stage, has accumulated £655.36.

The son who has taken the £1 million urges his brother to change his mind and tell his father he now wants to accept the £1 million instead. He argues that even if their father was to pro rate the amount and only give him half a million, it has to be a better option. Son 2 ignores his brother's advice.

It would be interesting at this stage to consider what choice you would have made at day one. I suspect I would have chosen the £1 million, since it just seems that the difference between £1 million and 1p is vast. Have a think about what amount you think Son 2 would have in his bank account at the end of the 31 days. As a reminder, at the end of each day the balance in the bank account is doubled.

At the end of 31 days, following the principle that the amount in the bank account is doubled each day, the balance for Son 2 would in fact have increased from 1p to in excess of **£10 million**. And yes, just as we did in the example about the credit card debt I'm going to repeat that in case you think it's a typo. It is, in fact, over **£10 million**.

I was so intrigued by this I actually calculated the figures myself. Yes, I know I'm a maths nerd, but for those who are interested, here's how the figures sit at the end of each day:

Day	Balance £
1	0.01
2	0.02
3	0.04
4	0.08
5	0.16
6	0.32
7	0.64
8	1.28
9	2.56

10	5.12
11	10.24
12	20.48
13	40.96
14	81.92
15	163.84
16	327.68
17	655.36
18	1,310.72
19	2,621.44
20	5,242.88
21	10,485.76
22	20,971.52
23	41,943.04
24	83,886.08
25	167,772.16
26	335,544.32
27	671,088.64
28	1,342,177.28
29	2,684,354.56
30	5,368,709.12
31	**£10,737,418.24**

What's really interesting is that right up until day 26, Son 2 has significantly less than the £1 million he could have taken at day one. It is only around day 27 that his balance starts to look anything like a comparable figure, and only on day 28 that it actually exceeds £1 million. After that, the numbers just sky rocket.

The principle to take from this is how easy it is not to bother saving small amounts, because it doesn't look as though anything's happening. BUT, if you do keep on saving, over time the numbers will really start to add up.

It's unlikely that you have a wealthy parent who will offer you 1p at day one with the promise to double what's in your bank account each day. However, don't let that be a reason not to take on board the principle involved.

The important thing to remember is that small savings over time can add up. At certain stages during the period the balance may be very small and often too small to think that it's worth continuing with. Over time, however, the amount can add up and really make a difference.

Think of, "From little acorns mighty oaks do grow."

Child benefit

Here's another more practical example, very appropriate for mothers.

Child benefit is currently £20.30 per week for your first child, payable from the date your child is born until they are aged 18, if they continue with full time education.

Suppose that, from the date your child is born, you invested that money on the stock market in a bundle of various stocks and shares. You then continued to invest the amount each week up until your child was aged 18.

What would that amount be worth if your investment grew at a rate of 10% each year?

If you did achieve a growth of 10% a year, at the date your son or daughter is aged 18 that amount would be worth £53,194.

Now, what could you do with that amount? It could fund your son or daughter through university, it could pay for a deposit on a flat, or it could fund a gap year.

Let's look at a different option.

Remember in the example above of the two sons, at day 18 the amount of money Son 2 had was just £1,310.72. This is a small sum comparison to the £10 million it had grown to by day 31.

Let's assume, in this example of child benefit, that instead of spending the money at age 18 you keep it invested and continue to receive 10% return each year. You don't add to the pot after your child's 18th birthday, since your child allowance stops at aged 18.

If you left £53,194 invested from aged 18 until your son or daughter was aged 65, and continued to receive 10% return each year, the money would then be worth a staggering £4,691,577.

What this is showing is that:

Every mother has the ability to ensure her child retires as a multi millionaire - if only she knew about this!

How realistic is a 10% return?

The above example uses 10% partly as a nice round figure, but also over the longer term this is not an unrealistic assumption. However, your actual return will depend totally on what stocks and shares you've invested in and the period of time that your money is invested.

The FTSE UK All Share Index is a reasonable yardstick to use to consider the growth in the value of the stock market, since it represents 98% of the market value of all shares on the UK Stock Exchange.

The base date for the index was 10th April 1962, with a starting value of 100, as a base.

As at the date of writing (May 2013), last night's closing value for the All Share Index was 3,473.99. That represents a compounded rate of return of circa 7% pa from the start date. Based on this, a 10% figure is not a completely unrealistic figure to work with. However, as with all averages, some years will have given a much lower return than 7%, and some will have given a much higher return.

Suppose the 10% figure turns out to be too optimistic and the growth rate is only 7%?

We'll use the same example of investing £20.30 per week from birth to age 18, and then leave the fund invested to age 65, not adding anything further to it after age 18. If the funds received a return of 5% pa, at age 65 the fund would then be worth (only!) £914,659.

If you were able to give your son or daughter an amount of **only** £914,659 (a figure just short of £1 million) when they reached age 65, do you think they'd be too disappointed?

What if you don't get child benefit?

The above example worked on the basis of child benefit being received for 18 years at the rate of £20.30 per week. Does this mean it's only relevant to those about to have their first child?

What if you don't receive child benefit? Maybe you don't have children, perhaps your children are grown up, or maybe you've just lost your child benefit because you earn over £60,000.

If you fall into any of these categories consider that the example was based on investing £20.30 per week, which is the equivalent of £2.90 per day.

If you don't receive child benefit the question you need to ask yourself is, "How can I find £2.90 per day to invest?" For anyone who frequents a coffee shop on a regular basis the answer is that this is very roughly the price of a coffee in the likes of Starbucks, Costa Coffee, etc.

If you don't drink coffee there will be many other ways to "find" enough savings within your spending habits. This will be addressed in more detail in Chapter 7 "In out, in out, shake it all about".

Child benefit is paid directly into the mother's bank account and I speak to a number of women who don't know off the top of their head how much it is. That's because it comes into the bank account and then typically it gets spent on general "stuff".

To ensure you are making best use of this money and saving it for the long term, make sure that you have a standing order or direct debit that moves this money straight into a savings vehicle. That way it won't just be spent on "stuff," but will instead be set aside for your son or daughter for a later age.

There will be some mothers who rely on this amount to help fund child expenses. However, so many mothers receive it and don't really know what it gets spent on. When you look at the figures above, it becomes obvious that this is such a waste.

What about inflation?

I have sometimes heard the comment that £4.7 million may sound like a lot of money now, but with inflation it won't be worth very much in 65 years.

Yes, this is a valid argument. If you take into account inflation, however, you also have to take into account the fact that it's likely that the £20.30 child benefit will also increase over the first 18 years too, to keep pace with inflation.

Let's assume child benefit increases roughly in line with inflation up until your child is age 18. If you assume that, between your child's 18th birthday and them reaching 65 years of age inflation is 5% pa, then an amount of £4,691,577 at age 65 years would be the equivalent of £473,611 at age 18.

Yes, of course it doesn't sound as attractive as £4.7 million, but I for one wouldn›t complain if someone were to give me the equivalent of £473,611 when I reach 65.

The important thing to take from this is the principle of saving on a regular basis, even if it's only a small amount. Don't get too hung up on the specifics of the numbers, it's the principle that's relevant.

There will be times when it will look as though the amounts may be too small to bother with. If you feel like this at any stage, go back and look at the example from "The Slight Edge". Your money won't be doubling overnight, as it did in this example, but the principle is still the same. Small amounts saved regularly over a long period and achieving a decent return can really add up.

How much should I save?

As a minimum, you should aim to save three months' worth of your normal essential expenditure. If you would typically spend £2,000 a month on essentials, aim to build up a cash reserve of £6,000. This should be in an account with easy access.

The rationale behind this is that, if you were to lose your job or have an unexpected significant expense, you would then have a cash reserve to cover that problem. Once you have built up three months' worth of expenses in this account you can then consider investing money over a longer term, either in a pension fund or an individual savings account (ISA).

What you've covered

Just as paying interest on interest (compounding) can seriously damage your wealth, earning interest on interest has an equal positive effect on your wealth.

Saving small amounts consistently over a long period of time, can add up to a sizeable pot. Think mighty oaks and little acorns!

Saving child benefit (or roughly the price of a cup of coffee each day) can allow your children to have a very decent sum when they retire. If you don't have children, look after yourself and save, so that you can benefit from your savings at a later age.

Action steps

Start saving now, even if it's just a small amount. If you're not a regular saver then this will help you start the saving habit.

Once you are already saving it is easier to increase the amount. For now, just take that first small step on your journey to being a wealthy woman.

If it's easier, start saving loose change in a glass bottle at the end of each day and watching it grow. Remember Savvy Sarah from Chapter 2 "A stitch in time". However, at the end of the month you must invest this amount, since you won't benefit from compounding by leaving your money in the bottle.

If you haven't saved up to now, this may be an easier way to start saving than to set up a standing order.

It's the first small steps that are important. Take that first step **TODAY**.

Chapter 7: In out, in out, shake it all about

"If God has allowed me to earn so much money, it is because He knows I give it all away..." - Edith Piaf

I'm sure you've all heard the saying, "Look after the pennies and the pounds will take care of themselves." I never understood what on earth it meant. I thought it meant that if I collected enough pennies then, somehow, miraculously I'd end up with a whole pile of pounds instead.

Now, many years later, I feel I do understand it. It's saying that if you watch the small items of expenditure this can often lead to much bigger savings.

I'm sure you have all promised yourself that: when you get a pay rise you'll start saving; when your business really takes off then you'll start saving; when you get that long awaited bonus you'll start saving. But, what happens?

All of a sudden, you find that the extra money is just getting spent, but you don't actually know what it's getting spent on. You just know that, despite the pay rise, there's still no money left in your account at the end of the month.

Expenditure creep

If you've ever heard the term "expenditure creep" then this is exactly what it is. Your expenditure seems to increase or "creep" up in line with your income. It often happens so automatically you don't even know you are doing it. You can't identify any specific increase in spending, and you look to see what large items you have purchased during the month. You can't think of anything, and looking through your bank statement and credit card statement doesn't show any large expenditure either.

In fact it's not the large items of spending you should be looking for: it's all the many smaller items of expenditure that you've bought without a second's thought. Each one on its own is very small - the new lipstick, the glossy magazine, or coffee and cake when you're a bit early for a meeting. You'd be surprised how quickly all these small items can add up to what is a reasonably large figure.

On more than one occasion I've actually got out my calculator and added up my credit card statement, convinced it was wrong. The number at the end seemed so big, but there was no significantly large item of spending in there. Lo, and behold! The computer was right and it was the much smaller figures added together that had caused the final total to look so disproportionately large.

What's the answer to this?

This is where you have to "look after the pennies and the pounds will take care of themselves."

To understand what you are spending your income on, and why you haven't got any money left at the end of the month to save, you need to start looking at exactly what it is the "pennies" are being spent on.

It sounds so obvious, doesn't it? Yet, like lots of obvious common sense nuggets of advice, you often need to be told it before the penny drops - excuse the pun.

If you are like one of the many females who feel they have no money left at the end of the month, but are not sure where on earth it's all disappeared to, then the good news is you're in good company - possibly even in the majority. The bad news is that, unless you do something about it now, you're heading for a very frugal lifestyle when you stop working.

If you haven't saved some money now, you're going to be brought up with a rather abrupt halt when you stop earning, because there's no pot of money at that stage to fund your purchases.

It's easy to think that when you get to retirement age you'll adjust your spending downwards, because you won't be at work anymore and some spending will reduce. It's true that commuter travel, spending on work clothes, and other work related expenses <u>will</u> reduce in value.

However, all of a sudden you have significantly more free time and your spending is likely to increase (or at least you'll want it to increase) on leisure activities. You may want to spend more time at your sports club, golf club or playing tennis. In fact if you've never had the time to join a sports club before, maybe now will be the period in your life when you do want to join, since all of a sudden you have the free time to enjoy it.

Sports clubs are not cheap, however. Not only that, but chances are that after your time at the gym/golf club/tennis club etc., you may want to have some lunch with friends. It's also the time when you'd like to take more holidays. Again, not cheap!

Have a think now about what you'd like your ideal day/week/month to be like when you're no longer working. Think about what level of spending you would need to have for that lifestyle.

Compare this to what your current investment and pension plans are likely to provide. If there's a large gap, you need to look at how you can save more now. Read on, to find out how.

Write it down

To understand where your money is going, you need to keep a detailed record of all your spending – and I do mean **all**. If you take cash out of the bank, spend that in what seems to be a very short period of time and subsequently take more cash out, then you need to understand exactly what that cash has been spent on.

Keeping a record of the fact that, for example, you spend £100 cash every week is of little use for budgeting purposes. This is because at the end of the month that's an amount in excess of £400 that has been spent on "stuff" and you still don't know what "stuff" you have bought.

You need to keep a **detailed record** of everything you are spending by:

- Direct debit
- Standing order
- Cheque
- Debit card
- Credit card
- Cash

For everything other than cash you can look through your bank statements and credit card statements to get an analysis. A number of banks and credit card companies provide some form of analysis on their statements, but do check to see if it's detailed enough.

The more detail you can provide, the easier it will be to see if there's a potential area of saving. Classifying something as "household" will not provide you with enough detail to plan accurately.

I have provided an example spreadsheet on my website which you may want to use at www.mary-waring.co.uk/TheWW-expenses/. It is quite detailed, but remember, the more detail you can provide at this stage the better.

The website spreadsheet has three separate tabs: expenses, income and cash flow. Complete the cells shaded yellow. Formulas have been included in the spreadsheet to calculate totals and average. Once you have completed the expenses and income figures the totals will automatically be carried forward to the cash flow sheet.

A copy of the spreadsheet in included as Appendix II. There is no colour shading in this version.

When you spend cash, make sure you either ask for a receipt, or carry around a little notebook in your handbag and record all that you are spending. Record it at the time you spend it. Don't wait until the end of the day, since if you do, there's a good chance you will have forgotten several purchases.

Sometimes, writing it down in advance of actually buying something can act as a bit of a brake on spending. Just the fact of having to write it down makes you think twice as to whether you really want to spend that amount, or not.

It's the same reason why slimming clubs ask you to write down what you're eating. Keeping a food diary helps you look back to see where your eating pattern could be improved. It also makes you think twice before you eat something and that may stop the chocolate éclair passing your lips in the first place.

Writing down your spending before you spend it works on the same principle. Think of it as weight watchers for your purse. If your spending is a bit overweight at the minute, a bit on the podgy side, well then it needs to be cut back until it's nice and lean.

At the end of each day, or end of each week, transfer your spending figures from the receipts and notebook onto the spreadsheet.

Your three month workout

You need to follow this regime for three months on average. If you did it for only a month, for example, you have no way of knowing how representative that month is. Did you spend less than average because you were monitoring it closely? Alternatively, was it a particularly expensive month because there were a number of birthdays, evenings out, parties, etc?

If you do it for a minimum of three months you can then start to see some patterns emerge. In addition, some utility bills may only be paid on a quarterly basis, so unless you do this exercise for three months, it may be unrepresentative of your typical spending.

What do you do once you have all this information?

Well you need to look at it, and look at it with a very critical eye. For every item on the list you should ask yourself, "Is it a necessary item of spending?" If it is, then the next question to ask is, "How can I reduce it?" Notice, I haven't asked the question "Can I reduce it?" Instead the question is, "How can I reduce it?" Start from the assumption that it is possible to reduce it. Asking the question this way will make your subconscious work in a way that is more likely to come up with an answer. Look at every single item on your list and see what can be done to reduce the amount you spend.

For example, if you spend a lot of money eating out at expensive restaurants, then consider reducing the number of times in the month that you eat out. Alternatively, consider going to a less expensive restaurant, at least on some occasions. However, do make sure you find a system that works well for you.

This means you need to find a system that allows you to still enjoy your social life, but also provides an opportunity to save.

The idea is to reduce your spending, but not to the extent that you become a hermit with no friends, no hobbies and no social life. You may end up with money in the bank, but you're unlikely to have much fun. This would not be sustainable over the long term. In fact, why would you want it to be?

Going out with friends and only ordering tap water, eating the free bread rolls and nothing else, may sound like a good way to save money. But, let's face it; is that really how you want to live? Your friends will soon abandon you.

Can you reduce it?

If you feel as though you're ready to jump in and tackle <u>every</u> item of spending, then go ahead.

However, I suggest you choose one area of expense at a time and see what you can do to get the level of spending down. The slow, steady approach may suit you better. Remember Aesop's fable of the tortoise and the hare. The tortoise started off slower, but won in the end.

Once you have that one area of expense reduced to a reasonably sustainable level going forward, look at the next area. It will take longer this way, but this is an exercise to follow on a consistent and regular basis: it's not a one-off exercise. It's certainly not a mad sprint to achieve something, which you then let slip because the effort to sustain that level is too great.

You'll be surprised how much scope there is for reducing your spending without it having a negative impact on your quality of life.

There are of course now so many helpful sites on the internet, and below are just a few examples. These are not necessarily the only ones or even the ones to be recommended. I have simply mentioned a few that spring to mind.

- www.uswitch.com will allow you to compare your utility prices.
- www.moneysupermarket.com will allow you to compare prices on a large number of different products and services.
- www.mysupermarket.co.uk will allow you to compare supermarket prices when shopping on line.

If there's a specific area where you're looking to save money, just put, "How do I save money on X?" into your search engine.

Do be aware though that a number of comparison sites are effectively advertising. They charge the company to be registered on the site, which means there may be a cheaper option from a company that isn't included. However, comparison sites are certainly a good starting place to see how much scope you may have to reduce the price you are currently paying for your service.

Shave a little... save a lot

What if there's no specific area where you think you can make some significant savings?

If this is the case, consider reducing a small amount from each item. Buy one less coffee a week; don't have a muffin each time you stop off for a coffee; eat in on one occasion a month, rather than always eating out. You'd be surprised how much all the little changes can add up.

To look at an example, let's assume you are earning an average salary of £25,000 pa. After tax and national insurance, that would net down to circa £1,500 per month take home pay. Let's assume that your spending is £1,400 per month, which means you therefore have disposable income of £100 at the end of the month.

Based on this, you decide that you haven't got sufficient disposable income to start saving, because maybe next month you'll have a large car expense, for example.

Just suppose, though, that over the next year you were able to increase your monthly income by 1% each month and reduce your monthly spend by 3% each month.

Both figures sound nice and small, not so great a change that it makes you feel you can't achieve it. If you did manage to increase your income by 1% a month and reduce your spending by 3% a month, then at the end of the year your disposable income of £100 per month will have increased to £719 per month.

Now, all of a sudden, that's a very significant figure and would certainly add greatly to your wealth if you saved this each month.

I do accept that at some point it becomes difficult to keep reducing your spending and keep increasing your income month on month. To start with, small changes are relatively easy to introduce, but as more time passes it becomes more and more difficult to make the changes.

However, the point I want you to take from this is that small changes are often ignored because you think they're not going to make enough difference to be worth bothering with. Don't forget, though, the example in Chapter 6 "Getting interesting" regarding the twin sons and the choice of £1 million or 1p: over time these small insignificant changes can really add up.

Keep making the small changes for as long as it's practical, and notice what difference it has made.

What about income?

The above example used the assumption you increase your income by 1% each month. However, if you're employed that's not necessarily such an easy thing to do.

Consider, though, what action you could take to help improve your pay rise at your next review. Are there some skills you can learn which will make you more valuable to your employer? Is there a course you can attend which will increase your skills base? If your existing employer does not have sufficient scope for advancement and promotion, why not consider what other opportunities are available elsewhere?

And what if you're self-employed?

Increasing your income doesn't necessarily have to mean working longer hours. That's not, in fact, acceptable to the majority of women who are desperately trying to find ways to reduce their working hours. What I'm suggesting, instead, is a case of working smarter not harder.

Consider, can you add a premium service to your offerings for some of your clients? Research has shown that 20% of your clients will pay a higher price for a premium service if it was available and offered. Think about what additional service you can offer your clients that will add significantly to your profit margin, without adding significantly to your hours.

If you provide a number of different services, consider what services can be bundled together so that the client spend is increased. If you are a coach and charge an hourly rate for a monthly coaching call, then a premium service may be the option of having a weekly email catch up in between calls.

This isn't ripping off your client. It's providing them with the extra service they want and for which they are willing to pay an additional sum.

It's the same principle that applies when Amazon tells you after you've bought an item, "people who bought this also bought ..." Personally, I find this useful. It's pointing me in the right direction of what other products I might like. Yes, of course I know it's increasing their profits, but it's also benefitting me. If I don't want to spend extra, then I just ignore these recommendations.

If you haven't got any ideas for how you can increase your income without increasing your working hours, find a good business coach. Your coach will be able to spot areas in your business where you can increase your profit without a disproportionate corresponding rise in the hours you need to work to achieve it.

Once is not enough

Performing the budgeting task above as a once off exercise is a great way to get you started. However, remember you need to do it on a frequent basis, since bad habits will creep back in over time.

I recommend you perform the budget exercise at least once a year and reassess what areas there are in your spending where there is potential to make saving.

What if you're one of those women who typically say, "But, I hate maths"?

If you think you hate maths and you're no good at it, then you need to change your thinking - and change it immediately. If you approach this with the attitude that you're going to hate the whole exercise and it will be a waste of time, then guess what? You will hate the exercise and will get very little benefit from it.

Instead, the way to approach it is to get yourself into a positive frame of mind. Sit down with the attitude that's it's a really good exercise for you to do to see where your hard earned cash is being spent, and where you can take some really positive steps to improve your wealth.

Maybe sit down with a nice glass of wine, or your favourite music playing in the background. View it as something to look forward to, in that you are really getting to grips with your finances. It's a necessary step to take in improving your financial position and helping you on your journey to be a wealthy woman.

Think about what you will gain at the end of the exercise and use this as your motivation. For those of us old enough to remember Jane Fonda, think of "no pain, no gain". If we could all achieve great wealth simply by wanting it and wishing it, then we'd all be rolling in money.

Back in the real world, if you want to achieve anything worth having, you have to put the effort in. Make sure you have a big enough dream and goal so that the achievement of your goal far outweighs the effort required to get there.

If you haven't yet done the exercise, go back to the SMART goal setting in Chapter 4 "And we're off". Making your goal relevant will drive you forward towards what you know you can achieve, if you keep working at it.

What you've covered

To control your spending you firstly need to know what your hard earned cash is being spent on.

Small changes in spending applied on a consistent and regular basis over a period of time can lead to large increases in your bank balance.

Small changes to your pricing, or alternatively bundling your services together, can increase your income at a disproportionate amount to the extra work required.

All this goes to show that if you look after the pennies, the pounds really can take care of themselves.

Action steps

From today, start to keep a record of everything you spend.

Look at each item and consider what you can do to reduce your spending.

If you're self-employed, consider how you can provide a premium service.

Consider whether you can bundle your services together, so that a client who would normally have purchased only one product or service will, instead, buy two.

If you're employed, consider what you can do to ensure a decent pay rise at your next review.

Enjoy the whole process! Don't view it as a terrible chore to be endured, but instead view it as a necessary step to take you to your desired goal of being a wealthy woman.

Chapter 8: Getting started: not too taxing

"Money is of value for what it buys, and in love it buys time, place, intimacy, comfort, and a private corner alone..." - Mae West

Congratulations you've now reached the stage of being ready to do something with your hard earned money. What should you do now that you've started to save?

The aim of this book isn't to teach you to invest, but to give you a deeper understanding of how to look after your finances and how to improve your wealth.

I had initially planned that the book would be very generic, so that no matter what country you are in, the advice would be relevant and applicable to you, regardless of your country's tax laws and regulations. For that reason my initial draft did not include any information on investing.

However, this chapter is for those readers in the UK who want a greater understanding of what they can do once they've successfully achieved the hard work of getting to grips with their finances and have now saved some money.

This chapter will not go into details as to how to choose the funds you want to invest in. Instead it will provide the basics of how a pension plan and an ISA (individual savings account) work and will hopefully encourage you to start saving into at least one of these two options.

Both have specific tax advantages. Which one is most appropriate for you depends on your priorities and circumstances. Use this chapter to provide the background you need, but then do talk to an adviser to determine the appropriate investment strategy that is right for you.

This chapter includes a lot of figures and is rather technical. Whilst I had planned that this book wouldn't be overly technical, it is impossible to explain the tax advantages of a pension and an ISA without delving into the details. Please bear with me.

If you find the figures complicated, don't get bogged down in trying to follow the calculations. Instead, accept that the figures are correct and aim to take on board the principle the figures are highlighting.

Some people (I'm one of them) like to see how the figures fit in to the theory, but for others the theory on its own will suffice. If you're not someone who wants to get to grips with the background numbers, don't let this put you off reading the chapter. Read the explanation, but concentrate on what the figures are showing you, rather than the details of how they are calculated.

How does a pension work?

Let's assume you want to invest £100 per month into your pension plan.

If you're a basic rate taxpayer paying tax at 20%, you actually pay in £80 per month from your bank account. The pension provider will then reclaim £20 from the tax office. This contribution comes from HM Revenue and Customs (HMRC).

When added to the £80 you invested from your bank account, this makes up your £100 contribution. The £20 from HMRC represents tax at 20% on the £100 gross amount you earned. In essence, the tax office gives you back the tax you suffered. Yes, in case you weren't aware of this, if you pay into a pension plan the tax office will refund into the plan the tax you had previously had deducted from your earnings.

The tax office rarely gives us money back, so you should all be taking advantage of this!

In short, you have paid in £80 and received £100 of value. Looks like a bargain to me!

Personally, I think all women's brains are hardwired to enjoy a bargain. Some women like to spend their money on shoes and handbags, some on books, others on theatre trips or holidays. Whatever your spending habit, we all enjoy getting good value.

Here you have what is, in effect, a 20% off sale, which runs on a permanent basis and yet so many of you are not taking advantage of it.

The position gets even better if you're a higher rate taxpayer paying tax at 40%. At the time of writing, that means you are earning in excess of circa £41,450.

If this is your situation, the process works as follows:

Like before, you pay in £80 and the tax office contributes £20 to make it up to your £100 monthly premium. However, when you complete your tax return and you note on your return your pension contributions, HMRC then recognises that to date you have only had 20% tax relief given, whereas you paid tax at 40%.

To bring your tax relief up to 40% the tax office will give you an extra £20 tax refund for each £80 you contribute.

Yes, you do actually get a reduction or refund of tax.

If you're up to date with your tax payments, then you will get a cheque in the post for £20 (or more likely it will be paid directly into your bank account). If you owe tax, this tax refund will be deducted from the amount you owe, reducing the amount you have to pay.

To summarise, you've initially paid £80 as a monthly premium, but then you receive £20 refund. The net amount you've paid is £60, but the gross amount into your pension pot is £100. In other words, you've received £100 of value, but it's only cost you £60.

If we said that the effect of these tax benefits for a basic rate taxpayer was the equivalent of a 20% off sale, then a 40% reduction is the equivalent of blue cross day! Don't miss out on this bargain - make sure you pay a regular pension contribution and receive your tax advantage.

A similar process will also be followed if you are a 45% taxpayer (earning over circa £159,440 at the time of writing). You pay in £55, but get £100 worth of value. If there was a 45% off sale in your favourite shop you'd be down there in a flash.

I know that contributing to a pension is never going to match the excitement you experience from spending on whatever it is that you like to spend your hard earned cash. However, if you concentrate on what good value you are getting, you will realise this is too good an opportunity to miss. Do not let it pass you by.

How much can you pay into your pension?

Under the current rules the amount you can pay in to your pension plan and receive tax benefits on is 100% of your earnings, subject to a maximum of £50,000 pa. (This maximum figure is reducing to £40,000 from April 2014.) For anyone who considers it impractical to make a pension contribution of the full amount you earn, consider what would happen if you were to receive an inheritance.

In this scenario, you may want to pay some of this into your pension. If you earned £40,000 and received an inheritance of £100,000, you could choose to pay £40,000 of the inheritance into a personal pension. Therefore, under these circumstances, paying in 100% of your earnings does not sound quite as ridiculous as it may seem at first.

The £50,000 current limit includes the additional basic rate tax relief. Therefore, a £50,000 gross contribution will cost you £40,000. The tax office will then provide a tax rebate of £10,000 to make the balance in your pension plan up to £50,000.

There are specific rules which allow you to use some of the earlier year's pension contribution limits if you haven't used your full contribution in these years. If you are looking to make a pension contribution, do talk to an independent financial adviser to ensure you are maximising your tax benefits.

What if you're self-employed?

We noted earlier that, if you are employed the maximum pension contribution, you can make to receive tax benefits is 100% of your earnings. If you're self-employed and trading as a sole trader the maximum pension contribution will be 100% of your pre-tax profits.

If you're self-employed and trading as a limited company the earnings limit is the amount you've received by way of **salary, but not dividend.**

For tax efficiency, directors who are employed through their limited company will often receive a reasonably small salary and the majority of their income will be received by way of dividend. This will limit the amount of personal pension contribution that can be made that will be eligible for tax allowances.

You can, in fact, make unlimited contribution to your pension plan, but the £50,000 limit (or the amount you earn if lower) relates to how much of your contribution will receive the tax benefits. If your contribution is in excess of this limit, the excess will not receive the tax advantages mentioned above.

If you're running your business through a limited company, the fact that your personal pension contribution can only receive tax advantages up to the amount you draw as salary does not mean that you can only make a very small contribution to your pension. You have an option to pay the pension contribution from your company, instead of paying it personally.

If the pension payment is paid from your limited company, the annual limit for tax benefits is £50,000 gross, regardless of how much you have drawn by way of salary. This will, therefore, allow you to make pension contributions in excess of the salary you receive, if you typically draw a small salary and receive the balance by way of dividend income.

The pension contribution paid by your company is tax deductible against your profits, so it will reduce your taxable profits and, therefore, reduce the corporation tax you pay.

In effect, a £10,000 pension contribution will reduce your taxable profits by £10,000 and therefore reduce your corporation tax bill by £2,000 at the small company rate of 20%. The net cost to a limited company of a £10,000 pension contribution is, therefore, £8,000.

When can you draw your pension?

Currently, you cannot access your private pension until you are aged 55. At that stage you can draw a maximum of 25% of the value tax free, and the balance will be used to provide an ongoing income.

The reason for these restrictions is that the tax advantages are to ensure you have money available for retirement. The government doesn't want the tax rules to be used as a means for you to save a nice wad of money courtesy of some lucrative tax advantages, which can then be used to fund your round the world trip. The concern would be that when you returned to the UK, you would then have no savings left and would need to rely on state support.

The tax advantages are there specifically to encourage you to save for your old age and not have to rely on the state. As a result, there are restrictions in place to ensure these funds are available for your retirement, rather than available purely as a savings balance.

Is your pension income taxable?

I am frequently asked this question since initial logic suggests that if you saved money in your pension plan from your earned income, and that money had been taxed, then you shouldn't be taxed twice.

But remember, as shown above, when you save money in your pension plan you get back the tax you suffered, so in effect you earned that money tax free. At the stage when you draw it, the income then becomes taxable. You are therefore only taxed once, although if you didn't know about the tax advantages it would feel as though you had suffered tax twice.

No national insurance contribution will be payable on your pension income once you are over state pension age, since NI payments cease once you have reached this age.

For most people, paying tax on pension income when they retire, and receiving a tax refund on pension contributions whilst they are working and contributing to a pension, will tend to work in their favour.

Often, you are paying tax at a higher rate when you are working than when you retire, since your earnings are higher whilst during your working life. Research has shown that four out of five people who are higher rate taxpayers when they are working, are then basic rate taxpayers when they retire. (At the time of writing the limit of earnings as a basic rate taxpayer are up to circa £41,450).

To see the effect of this, let's look at an example. Let's assume you are a 40% taxpayer when you contribute to your pension and a 20% taxpayer when you receive your pension income.

If you are a higher rate taxpayer when you contribute to the pension plan, each £100 payable into your pension savings will cost you £60. The pension fund you have invested in will, hopefully, grow in value. The growth in the fund will not suffer capital gains tax and, with the exception of the 10% tax deducted from dividends, the fund will also be free of income tax. However, to make the example easier let's assume that there's no growth in the fund at all.

When you reach retirement age and draw your £100, the income you will receive is split into firstly, 25% which is tax free, and the remaining 75% balance, which is subject to income tax.

Therefore, for a basic rate taxpayer paying tax at 20%, for each £100 drawn from the pension plan you will receive:

- £25 (25% of £100), which will be tax free.
- The balance of £75 will be taxed at 20%. This will net to £60 after tax.

Therefore, the net amount (after tax) you will receive from your pension for each £100 drawn is £85 (£25 tax free and £60 after tax of the balance).

However, remember that in the example above, we've shown that as a higher rate taxpayer the £100 into your pension cost you £60.

Even if you allow for no growth in your pension fund at all, the £60 paid in is equivalent to £85 when it's drawn. This is a return of 42% even before you take growth into account.

The example above has shown that, if you are a higher rate taxpayer when you make a pension contribution and a basic rate taxpayer when you draw the pension income, you have benefitted financially from the difference in tax rates.

What if you're one of the one in five people who is a higher rate taxpayer when you draw your pension?

If you're a higher rate taxpayer when you draw your income, and we assume that your entire pension was to be taxed at 40%, the amount you will receive from each £100 drawn is:

- £25 (25% of £100), which will be tax free, as above.
- The balance of £75 will be taxed at 40%. This will net to £45 after tax.

Therefore, as a higher rate taxpayer, the net amount you will receive from your pension for each £100 drawn is £70 (£25 tax free and £45 after tax of the balance).

For each £100 paid into your pension plan the cost to you was £60, after your 40% tax benefit. Therefore, you pay in £60 and receive back £70, even allowing for no growth in the funds that your pension is invested in. This is a return of 17%.

In practice, the return will be somewhere between 17% calculated above and the 42% calculated for a basic rate taxpayer. This is because, in the above example we assumed you pay tax at 40% on the full amount of your pension, whereas in practice the first £9,440 is tax free and the next £32,020 will be taxed at 20%. Only the balance in excess of this is taxed at 40%.

This shows that there are various tax advantages to be had by saving money on a regular basis into a pension plan. Since the government so rarely give us anything for free, it would be a shame to miss out. Do make sure you take advantage of it.

In view of what you›ve learnt about pensions, the next time someone tells you that pensions are either complicated or boring, you can put them right - pensions are like a 20% off sale.

That makes them neither complicated, nor boring!

Individual savings account (ISA)

Having looked in detail at pensions, the other area we will now look at is ISAs – individual savings accounts.

In an effort to get us all saving as much as possible the government allows tax advantages when saving into an ISA. Annual limits are set as to what amount you can save into an ISA each year and receive the tax benefits. These tax benefits are explained in detail below.

Ordinarily, if you invest in the stock market and your investment increases in value (which of course you hope it will), you would suffer capital gains tax on the increase. For example, if you invested £40,000 into a stocks and shares portfolio and that grew, over time, to £80,000, you would have made a capital gain of £40,000. Under the current limits, £10,900 of this gain is not subject to a tax charge. The balance of £29,100 will be taxed at 18%, or 28%, depending on whether you are a basic rate or higher rate taxpayer. Therefore, the tax charge will be between £5,328 and £8,148.

However, if the £40,000 had been invested over a number of years in various ISAs the £40,000 gain would be totally tax free. As a result, you would have additional cash of between £5,328 and £8,148 depending on your tax position.

In addition, if you invested outside an ISA plan, you would suffer income tax if you received interest or dividends from your investments.

However, within an ISA environment no tax is suffered - neither income tax nor capital gains tax. The one exception, as mentioned above under pensions, is that the 10% tax suffered on a dividend cannot be reclaimed.

The limits for 2013/14 for how much you can save into an ISA are £5,760 for a cash ISA, or £11,520 for a stocks and shares ISA. This means you can invest up to £5,760 in a cash ISA and then the balance of up to £11,520 in total in a stocks and shares ISA.

For example, you may choose to invest £4,000 in a cash ISA and then £7,520 in a stocks and shares ISA, or you may chose to invest the full amount in the stocks and shares ISA with no amount in a cash ISA.

We are each given a new allowance each tax year, which runs from 6th April in one year to 5th April in the following year. In each tax year you can only have one cash ISA and one stocks and shares ISA. However, from the following tax year you can open up new

ISAs with new providers. There is no reason why the new ISA in the following tax year must be with the same provider as your existing ISA.

In relation to tax benefits, an ISA is effectively the mirror image of a pension. Under the pension rules the amount paid in on a monthly basis is grossed up (e.g. the basic rate taxpayer pays in £80 and it is grossed up to £100.) Then, at a later stage when the money is drawn, 25% is tax free and the balance is taxable.

Under an ISA contribution, there is no tax advantage when the money is paid in. If you want to make £100 contribution to your ISA plan it will cost you £100. However, when you draw from the ISA the full amount of all money drawn is tax free.

An ISA does not have the same restriction as a pension regarding how much you can draw from it and when you can draw the income. If you wanted to take the full amount out of your ISA savings and go on a round the world cruise, there is nothing to stop you. As noted above, you cannot access your private pension at all until aged 55. Then, at that age, you can draw a maximum of 25% of the fund tax free and the balance will be used to provide an ongoing income.

Pension or ISA?

In an ideal world you would want to have <u>both</u> an ISA savings plan and a pension plan to take full advantage of the tax allowances available for each. The ISA allowance is a "use it or lose it" allowance. If you don't use your allowance this year, the allowance is lost. You won't get a double allowance next year if you haven't used it. Unlike the pension allowance, it cannot get carried forward for any period of time.

Therefore, to ensure you take full advantage of tax free savings in an ISA, do make sure you use your allowance each year.

What you've covered

There are various tax advantages for investing into both an ISA savings plan and a pension plan.

A pension plan provides tax benefits when you pay into the plan by grossing up your contribution for the tax suffered. When the income is drawn from the pension it is taxable at that stage.

An ISA doesn't give tax benefits when you make the contribution: £100 invested in your ISA will cost £100. However, the income is wholly tax free when it is drawn.

In an ideal world you would have both a pension and an ISA to make sure you are getting your full tax advantages.

A pension is effectively a 20% off sale if you are a basic rate taxpayer. If you›re a higher rate taxpayer, it's the equivalent of blue cross day at the sales! *What is there to not like about that?*

Action steps

Review the cash flow prepared as part of the action step in Chapter 7 "In out, in out, shake it all about". Consider what savings can be identified to go towards a regular monthly contribution into an ISA savings plan or a pension plan.

Do not lose out on these important tax advantages.

If you spend a reasonable sum in the coffee shop on a regular basis, consider whether you'd prefer to invest this amount rather than purchase coffee and cake. Good for both your financial future and your waistline!

If you retire at 65, you will hopefully live for another 20-25 years. It's going to be a very difficult time if you have insufficient funds to enjoy your retirement. Review the lifestyle of Sarah, first introduced in Chapter 1 "Because you're worth it", against the lifestyle of Nicola. Which lifestyle do you prefer?

Pay particular attention to the details in Chapter 2 "A stitch in time," which highlighted how Sarah and Nicola's lives diverge as they get older and approach retirement age. Decide which lifestyle is the one you want and take the necessary action **now** to plan for that lifestyle.

Chapter 9: Wealthy woman wobbles

"Obstacles are put in our way to see if we really want something, or just thought we did..." - Alyssa Farmer

Now that you've read this far in the book, learnt all that you have learnt, and completed the action steps, does it mean that everything will be plain sailing from now on?

I would love to be able to tell you, "yes", but unfortunately the honest answer is, "no." Despite how well you have followed the advice, things may still go wrong. In fact, it would be safer to assume that they <u>will</u> go wrong, and plan for what you will do in that eventuality. This way, if you do hit a problem it won't be such a shock for you, and you will have a strategy in place to deal with the issue.

Don't put yourself in a position where a small unexpected set back knocks you so off course that you give up on your journey to be a wealthy woman. If you have planned for what will happen in a worst-case scenario, you will be more likely to pick yourself up and deal with the setback.

Yes, it will mean that your plan may not be achieved exactly as you had wanted. But, much better that you recognise this and revise your plan, rather than be so despondent you just give up.

What you must remember is that everything shown throughout this book is a long term process to follow. As I said very early on, this isn't a get rich quick scheme. Of course, it will be very disappointing if after all your hard work something does go wrong, but unfortunately that's just life. Things happen that you hadn't expected or planned for, which have the power to derail us. The important thing to do is to learn from the experience, pick yourself up and "get back on the horse".

This chapter will therefore look at what can go wrong, what this may mean for you and your plans and what action you can take to deal with it. Since there are various things outside of your control that may impact on your journey to be a wealthy woman, I have nicknamed these setbacks "wealthy woman wobbles."

Wealthy woman wobble: You lose your job

If you lose your job this will have a major impact on your ability to save and to follow your original plan, unless you secure another new employed role very quickly. If you are out of work for any period of time, it will therefore mean that it's very likely you will not reach the net worth goal you had set for yourself for the next period. That's the bad news.

However, the good news is that, if you've followed the plan closely, you will have some funds set aside in a savings account to help you through this period. As mentioned in Chapter 6 "Getting interesting", it's always important to have some emergency cash, a "rainy day fund" for such an eventuality. A safety net of three to six months' worth of your expenses is recommended. For example, if your typical monthly expenses total £2,000, aim to build up a minimum of £6,000 in an emergency account which has immediate access.

This money can then be used if you were to lose your job. You can then dip into it to cover your monthly living expenses until you have a new position.

In an ideal world, you hopefully won't be out of work for too long and it won't make too much of a dent in your plans. Once you are back in employment, your main priority is then to build the emergency fund back up to its previous level. If you do need to dip into this pot you will be very grateful that you started saving. Always aim to be a

Savvy Sarah, rather than a Not-so-savvy Nicola.

Instead of worrying about the fact that your plans have now gone off course, be thankful that you took the advice to start saving. This has now provided you with a buffer to see you through your period of not earning.

You never know, losing your job could actually be a boost to your plans. What if you received a redundancy package and then managed to secure a new role quite quickly? In this instance, at least part of your redundancy income can be committed towards your long term wealth plans. It may bring your "wealthy woman" status a lot closer and help you achieve your plans quicker than you had expected.

The important thing to do if you do lose your job is to concentrate on your short term priority of finding a new role. Do not worry about what this has done to your long term plans. Certainly, don't go out and have a major shopping spree to make you feel better! Retail therapy will provide only a very short term boost, and the impact on your finances of having a spending spree could be disastrous.

If you haven't been keeping the budgeting exercise up to date, go back and do the income and expenditure exercise in Chapter 7 "In out, in out, shake it all about" and see what expense items you can reduce. There will now be even greater incentive to reduce the expense, and this may well highlight areas of saving that you hadn't identified when you first completed the exercise.

It's amazing how focused and inventive we can all become when necessary. You've probably heard the phrase, "Necessity is the mother of invention". This means difficult situations will inspire ingenious solutions in order to get rid of, or at least reduce, the difficulty.

What may have looked like a reasonably tight budget when you last completed the exercise may now have further areas of saving, when you review it with greater urgency to reduce your expenses.

Once you are back in employment, revisit the net worth exercise in Chapter 4 "And we're off" and reconsider what your SMART goals should now be for the next six months. It may be that your original plan has been set back by a few months. Remember, what you're concentrating on is the long term goal, rather than any short term achievement. Focus on achieving your next six month target and don't concentrate on the fact that you've missed your original short term goal.

Wealthy woman wobble: You lose a major client

This will potentially have the same impact for a self-employed individual as the impact of an employee losing her job. The extent of the impact will depend on how large a dent the loss of the client makes in your cashflow, and how quickly you can replace the lost income.

The way to deal with this wealthy woman wobble is to follow the same advice as set out for the employee who loses her job in the wealthy woman wobble, above.

Use your emergency cash fund to tide you over while you find ways to replace the lost income. If, during this period, you are no longer adding to your cash reserves, but are instead drawing on them, that's okay, since that's exactly why they're there. Be thankful you've been sensible enough to build up a reserve.

As above, go through your expenses with a fine tooth comb and see what other areas of saving there may be. Even if you performed this exercise quite recently, I bet you'll find additional savings, now that your income has reduced, and have made cost cutting more of a priority.

Once your income is back on track, rebuild your emergency cash reserves and rework your six month SMART goals for your next net worth target.

Wealthy woman wobble: You have a major unplanned expense

No matter how careful you are with monitoring your expenses, there will often be unplanned costs that arise. For example, your car may need a repair, your property may need some major maintenance, or you may have a large dental bill. The last example is based on personal experience, having cracked a tooth last week and just been advised by the dentist what the cost will be for the necessary dental repair work. Enough to make me feel quite faint!

If some unplanned expense does arise, you will hopefully have enough money set aside in your "rainy day fund" to cover this. Depending on the size of the expense, it could potentially make a very large dent in the fund. If it does, that's okay, because this is exactly what the fund is meant to cover.

Having reduced the fund to cover the unplanned expense, your priority is then to concentrate on building it up again, back to its original level.

What if you don't have sufficient in your reserve fund to cover the expense? If the expense arises at a time when you are just building up your fund, or maybe you've just drawn on it to cover a shortfall in your income, potentially there isn't enough in your "rainy day fund" to cover the expense.

In this instance, you will probably have to use a credit card and recognise that it may take a few months to pay off the balance. Having seen the figure in Chapter 5 "Till debt us do part" you will understand how much this is going to cost you. If this is the exception, rather than the rule, it shouldn't cause too great a problem. However, do make sure you are applying these principles to essential expenses and not expense items that can wait until you have saved sufficient to cover the cost.

Having used your credit card, make a concerted effort to get the balance paid off as quickly as possible. This will be a good time to look for a credit card with a 0% introductory offer for purchases. If you can put your purchase on this credit card it will give you possibly six months to get it repaid before any interest charges kick in.

Do plan your budget, so that you can get the balance paid off during the interest free period, otherwise the interest charges will seriously mount up. Certainly don't be tempted to buy anything else on this card simply because you have the capacity on your credit limit. Any new card you acquire is for the emergency expense only. Remember, this is only to cover a wealthy woman wobble.

Wealthy woman wobble: Tax laws change

Chapter 8 "Getting started, not too taxing" explained the current tax benefits surrounding saving into an ISA and a pension plan. One thing to bear in mind is that at any stage the government may reduce or remove these benefits.

Personally, I think it's unlikely the benefits will be fully removed, since the government is desperate for us all to start saving more towards our old age to ensure we're not relying on state support when we retire. However, it is, of course, possible that some of the additional benefits available to higher rate taxpayers may be reduced, so that they do not receive any greater tax benefits than basic rate taxpayers.

If this happens there's very little you can do to change it. However, even if changes are introduced, what you can do is look at exactly what savings and pensions you currently have in place and make sure you are making the most of the tax advantages available.

You can't change tax policy, but you can ensure you are receiving the best benefit with your savings and investment plans from all the possible benefits that are on offer. Since that's the area you have control over, make this the area you concentrate on.

Speak to your accountant and IFA (Independent Financial Adviser) to enquire what you can do to improve your financial position.

Wealthy woman wobble: You get divorced

Divorce will cause not just emotional upset, but financial upset too. No matter what your personal and financial circumstances are prior to divorce, it's very possible that after the divorce your financial situation will have deteriorated. The income coming into the family during marriage, which covered one house and one lot of household expenses, will now be used to cover two houses and two lots of household expenses. Even if there appears to be sufficient funds to adequately cover the needs of both parties, the same level of income will still be spread more thinly. This is bound to have an impact.

If you are going through divorce, or have recently gone through divorce, go back and rework your income and expenditure exercise and see where you can shave some costs. Depending on your circumstances, this may now become an urgent task. However, if you have been keeping track of your spending as discussed in Chapter 7 "In out, in out, shake it all about", you will have all the data necessary to consider what changes you can make.

Having completed the income and expenditure exercise, rework your SMART goals. Potentially, your net worth target may need to be reduced in the short term. However, as I've said before it's the longer term goal that is important, not a short term achievement.

If divorce has led to a change in financial circumstances, then your SMART goals need to be reviewed. There's no point in working towards a goal which you now know is unlikely to be met. This will only set you up for disappointment.

The aim of setting a goal and pushing yourself to achieve it is to get as close as possible to it, provided you exert a huge effort. If you know from the start you are unlikely to meet it, then there is very little incentive to try at all.

If your financial circumstances change permanently, do make sure this is reflected in updated SMART goals.

Very often in a marriage or partnership, one person deals with the joint finances. If, prior to reading this book, you were the one who didn't get involved in finances and left that task to your partner, hopefully you are now more comfortable with looking after your money and feel confident you are able to plan. This will hold you in good stead for the future.

If you are feeling a bit unsure, or feel you are lacking in confidence, go back through the book again. Reread the relevant chapters and then do the action steps. Concentrate on one area at a time until you begin to feel more comfortable and confident with that area, and then move onto the next.

There is nothing to stop you gaining control of your finances and being able to plan for the future.

Wealthy woman wobble: The stock market falls.

An important thing to be aware of when investing in the stock market is that stocks will not only go up, but may also fall. Reviewing the figures for any stock market index over even a short period of time will highlight this.

There are often periods of sharp or sustained rises, followed by drops. As the market starts to rise, investors become more confident and it encourages others to invest. At some point some investors want to crystallise their gain and may start to sell. Following the normal rules of supply and demand, prices will then fall.

Often, as followers of herd mentality, some of those who invested on the upward trend now start to feel uncomfortable with the fall and decide to sell. This brings the price down even further.

The main thing to realise when investing on the stock market is that if the market falls, it doesn't mean the whole plan doesn't work. If you don't plan to sell your investments at this stage, any loss is purely a paper loss. Yes, it feels very uncomfortable and it hurts, since you become very aware that your hard work in saving has now generated a loss. Even if it is just a paper loss, it still does not make for a warm, fuzzy feeling.

However, the thing to remember is that what has been shown in this book is a long term process. This book is not designed to show you how to buy low, sell high. That is effectively gambling, which isn't what this book is all about.

Don't be tempted to try to time the market - this is futile. We all know that the way to make a short term gain is to buy low and sell high. The problem is no one can time the market accurately enough to know when the market is at its lowest and when it's at its highest.

A study performed at the beginning of 2008 asked a number of experts what they predicted the FTSE 100 would be at the end of the year. The FTSE 100 is the index of the top 100 companies listed on The London Stock Exchange by market capitalization: (the number of shares issued multiplied by the share price).

Here are their predictions:

Lehman Brothers	7300
Lewis Charles Securities	7200
Gartmore	7200
UBS	6960
Hargreaves Landsdown	6900
Capital Spreads	6800
Seven Investment	6413

How close were they?

Well, at the end of 2008 the actual figure was 4434.

If the experts can get it so wrong, what chance do the rest of us have?

Another study carried out by *Financial Times Money* in November 2010 highlighted that non-professional investors trying to time the market were, on average, losing 1.2% per annum. Over 18 years they were typically down 20%, compared to the alternative of simply leaving their money invested in the market.

The study shows that if you invested £1,000 in the FTSE All Share in October 2000, it would have grown to £1,330 during the following 10 year period. (The FTSE UK All Share Index is a reasonable yardstick to use to consider the growth in the value of the stock market, since it represents 98% of the market value of UK shares on the Stock Exchange).

However, if instead of leaving the money invested for the whole period you missed the best 10 days over the same 10 year period, it would be worth £720. If you missed the top 20 days, it would be worth just £474. Therefore, missing just 20 days out of 3,650 days would result in your investments being worth about a third of the figure it would have been if you had left the money invested.

What this proves is that <u>trying to time the market is futile</u>. Don't be tempted to sell your investments if the market falls. Instead, have a long term investment strategy discussed and agreed with your IFA. The principles will apply for both when the market rises and also when it falls.

What you've covered

What this chapter has shown is that things <u>will</u> go wrong, and it's very likely you will have a wobble (and more likely more than one wobble) on your journey to be a wealthy woman. Recognise this from the outset, so that you can plan for this and won't be tempted to give up if and when this does happen.

Any deviation from plan is only a temporary setback. It doesn't mean the process doesn't work, and certainly doesn't mean you should give up altogether.

You may need to change your long term goal since your change in circumstances may mean that you now cannot achieve the initial goal you had set. But, that's the whole point of setting SMART goals and re-evaluating them at six month intervals.

If your long term goal is no longer appropriate for whatever reason, then <u>change</u> your goal. <u>Don't give up on it.</u>

Action steps

If you experience a wealthy woman wobble, go back to the principles discussed earlier in the book:

Check your expenses and see where there are savings to be made. Even if you did the exercise relatively recently, following a change in circumstances you may find savings you hadn't considered before. Remember the saying, "necessity is the mother of invention".

If necessary, use your credit card for a major unexpected (but necessary) expense. This is certainly one of the times when a credit card really is your flexible friend. If possible, get a credit card with an interest free period for a time to improve your budgeting and save interest.

Rework your SMART goals. It may be that the unexpected has knocked you off your initial course. If it does, rework your new figures and then put all your effort into achieving the revised target.

Recognise now what other issues specific to your circumstances may knock you off course and disrupt your plans. Consider in advance what you will do if this were to occur. Whether or not you were a girl guide, live by the motto, "Be prepared".

Chapter 10: The new you

"A woman's best protection is a little money of her own..." - Clare Boothe Luce

Congratulations! If you've read all the chapters up to now, and completed the action steps, you will certainly be well on your journey to becoming a wealthy woman.

If you haven't completed the action steps yet, but used your first read of the book to get a general overview, now is the time to go back to each chapter, reread it and complete the tasks. Even if you're convinced you can easily do it, do make sure you spend the time actually doing it. It's one thing to know what to do and another thing to actually get on and do it. It's often only in the doing that you realise something isn't quite as clear as you had previously thought.

Everything shown in this book is a "roadmap" - a step-by-step process to take you to where you want to go. The aim is to follow each of the small steps that will move you forwards towards your goal, even though sometimes it may seem that you are not making significant progress.

Remember the example of "The Slight Edge" - each action is small enough to make it very easy to do. However, the flip side to this is that each action is also small enough to make it easy NOT to do, since the impact of not doing it is very small in the short term.

All the action steps need to be in place as a process to follow on a regular basis. After a while, they will become so ingrained and such a habit that you will follow them automatically, without having to think too much about it. To start with, you will have to work hard to get them to become habits. If you start to get out of your comfort zone and feel decidedly awkward, well good! This is a sign that your old habits are changing and your future is about to change, too.

"The new you" chapter has been designed as a "tick box" for you to gauge how many of the action steps you have performed to date, and how far you have come on your journey to become a wealthy woman. I have listed below all the things I hope you have learnt from reading the book. Go through each of the points and tick whether it applies to "the new you". If it doesn't yet, and you haven't completed all of the action steps, or haven't completed them fully, go back, reread the relevant chapter and concentrate on doing the necessary steps until you can tick the box.

Then, on a regular basis, perform the whole exercise again to ensure your old habits haven't crept back in. Think of it as a money MOT.

How often you need to do this will depend on your own specific circumstances. If you have started from a place of having very little knowledge of what your money is being spent on, and have very little control over how you spend it, you will need to check in on a weekly or maybe even a daily basis.

Once you are more in control you may want to reduce this to a monthly MOT. No matter how much you feel in control of your finances, do make sure you always perform the MOT at least on an annual basis.

When you take your car for an MOT it's partly because you are legally obliged to do so, but it's also to ensure that if there is a problem with your car you become aware of it while it's still a small problem. At this stage, it's much easier (and cheaper) to rectify than when it's become a much more serious issue. The same principle is true for dealing with your wealth.

Go through all the exercises at least once a year. If there are areas where you realise you've let things slip, then concentrate on these areas and monitor these specific issues on a regular basis.

So, here goes. Below are the areas where I would like you to be able to say, "yes" to all the comments shown.

Net worth

Yes, I've downloaded the net worth spreadsheet from www.mary-waring.co.uk/TheWW-networth/ and I've completed my current net worth at least on a "best guess" basis. I've set my SMART goals for what I want my net worth to be at the end of the next six months, and I've set a reminder in my diary system to check my achievement against my goal in six months time.

The goal is a bit of a "knee trembling" goal, but I've decided that if I'm going to do it at all, I may as well go for it. I'm confident I can achieve the goal with focus, hard work and commitment. I spend some time each day imagining I have already achieved my goal. Sometimes, it seems so real I can almost see it.

I'm recalculating my net worth every six months and looking at where I am in relation to the goal I've set. I use this as a learning exercise and don't beat myself up if I haven't achieved the goal. If I've exceeded my target, I give myself a big pat on the back.

Saving

Yes, I'm determined not to put off saving any longer. I had always thought that I'd leave saving until I had a pay rise and had some extra cash, but I now recognise that there will be lots of calls on my cash at every age and it doesn't necessarily get easier as I get older, or earn more money.

I've started saving on a regular basis, even when it's just a small amount. After a number of years of not saving, it has made me feel a little bit uncomfortable, but I want to "just do it". Now that I've started, I plan to review the monthly savings figure regularly, with the aim of increasing the monthly savings amount as soon as my budget will allow. Whenever I get a pay rise or bonus I will ensure I also increase my monthly savings figure.

I'm going to start my "rainy day fund" immediately and keep contributing to it until the balance is equivalent to three months' worth of my expenses. Once my emergency fund is up to the right level, I can then direct my monthly savings to an ISA.

I'm aware this is a long term savings plan, so will not be dipping into it when I fancy a new pair of shoes, a trip to the theatre, or some other lovely goodies that I have my eye on. When I want these goodies, I will save up for them until I can afford to purchase them.

Pension

Yes, I've joined my employer's pension scheme, since I realise that with my employer and the government willing to contribute to it if I do, it would be foolish not to take advantage of this. I recognise state pension age for women is currently increasing and is likely to continue to do so. This emphasises the need to have my own plan, so I can stop work or reduce my hours when it suits me - not when the government says I can.

Yes, I'm self-employed and don't have access to an employer funded pension scheme, but I haven't used this as an excuse not to get started. I may not have an employer contribution, but I can still get a government contribution. I certainly don't want to miss out on that.

I've looked at the lifestyle I'd like to lead when I retire and worked out how much income I'll need each year as a minimum. Obviously, anything in excess of this will be nice, too! With the help of my IFA I know what size pension fund I need to achieve this, and how much I should be saving into my pension plan each month. It's not always easy and sometimes it means I have to cut back on my spending to be able to afford it. However, the thought of being in the same position as Not-so-savvy Nicola keeps me going. I definitely do not want to still be working in my 70s through necessity because I haven't planned at an early age.

Credit card

Yes, I'm in control of spending on my credit card and I know exactly how much interest my credit card company is charging me. I no longer panic when my credit card statement arrives, and nor do I leave the bill unopened on the basis I'd prefer not to know how much I'm spending.

Prior to reading this book I had foolishly built up large credit card balances. I can say "foolishly", now that I know the impact over time of paying off just the minimum monthly payment. I'm horrified by the example of how long it would take to get my credit card bill repaid by paying just the minimum each month. Now that I realise, I have a plan to reduce my current credit card balance. Although this may take some time, I recognise that each small step will take me towards my ultimate goal of being a wealthy woman.

I won't put any purchase on my credit card that I can't afford to pay off immediately.

For at least one month I'm only going to purchase things using a debit card or cash, so I can compare how much I spend this way, compared to how much I would normally spend using my credit card. Who knows, this may now become the norm for me.

In future I'm going to look at how much something costs in total, rather than how much I will pay back each month. I've fooled myself up to now that my credit card balance isn't costing me too much, but now I'm aware of just how expensive it is and I don't want to follow that example any more.

Budgeting

Yes, I've started the three month exercise of seeing exactly what I'm spending my money on. I will then go through each item and see how my spending can be reduced or removed. If there's no big expense item to look at, I realise that saving a small amount from each expense item will work, too.

Having dealt with my expenses, I'm going to brainstorm how I may be able to increase my income - without having to work longer hours.

I'll revisit these exercises regularly, since I know bad habits can creep back in very easily.

I'm going to follow the spreadsheet on www.mary-waring.co.uk/TheWW-expenses/ and amend it to suit my circumstances. Once I've done the hard work at the beginning of getting the spreadsheet set up, I know it's going to be a lot easier on an ongoing basis. If I make sure I get into a habit, it will then become second nature to write down all I spend and monitor it closely.

Summary: The new you

What constitutes being a wealthy woman will mean different things to different people. It doesn't necessarily mean "rolling in it" and having so much money that you'll enter *The Times* 'rich list'. It may simply mean you feel confident you will have the amount you need to do the things you'd like to do in the future, no matter how lavish or frugal a lifestyle you plan to lead.

For some, it will mean financial freedom, so you no longer have to work. For others, it will mean you no longer panic during the last week of the month that your income is about to run out.

So, yes, I have started on my journey to become a wealthy woman.

I've taken control of planning for my future. I recognise it's my responsibility to look after my finances, since I know "a man is not a financial plan." I realise I have to make saving and planning for my future one of my priorities if it's ever going to happen, and so I'm not going to delay it any further. If I don't start planning now, potentially I will be working well past my preferred retirement date, and that thought makes me shudder. I realise that relying on the state to support me when I'm older is not a good plan.

I've shared my plans with my friends/husband/partner and they are all fully on board to support me in this. I'm prepared to make a few small short term sacrifices with a view to improving my long term situation. Sometimes I will eat in with friends, rather than going to a swanky wine bar and blowing a great wad of cash. Since I've shared my plans with my friends, they will support me in this. In fact a few of my girlfriends are planning to follow my example.

I've reread the stories of Savvy Sarah and would much prefer to be like her in later life, than end up scrimping and struggling, like Not-so-savvy Nicola.

I tell all my girlfriends that it's possible to get to grips with your finances no matter how little control you had over your money initially. I managed to do it, so no reason why they can't.

I'm aware of the comment by Madeleine Albright, former US Secretary of State, "There is a special place in hell for women who don't help other women"[2]. I've seen the example from "The Slight Edge" and recognise that just because something takes a while to achieve, it doesn't mean I'm not going to get there. I am!

I recognise things may go wrong along the way, but what I also know is that, if something does go wrong, the worst this can do is to potentially shift my plan back by a few months. It doesn't mean that the plan doesn't work and should be abandoned.

---

2 (Made at a Keynote speech at "Celebrating Inspiration" luncheon with the WNBA's All-Decade Team, quoted in Mechelle Voepel, ESPN (July 13,2006).

I've committed to going through all the action steps in the book on a regular basis to keep me on track.

I enjoy taking control of my finances and planning for the future. It's much better to be in control of my money, rather than my money to be in control of me. Despite all my uncertainties and my lack of confidence when I picked up this book, I am thoroughly enjoying my journey to become a wealthy woman.

I do hope you've enjoyed reading the book and have gained some really good tips about how to progress on your journey to be a wealthy woman.

No matter where you are on your journey: whether you're just starting out, or whether you have now completed your journey and can say, "I am a wealthy woman", please do email me at Mary@mary-waring.co.uk to let me know how you are getting on. Let me know what advice in the book has been the most influential in improving your wealth. Which action steps have you now introduced into your habits that you believe have really changed how you view your finances and plan for the future?

Finally, remember the words of Madeleine Albright: "There is a special place in hell for women who don't help other women." If you know a woman who needs help with her finances, please tell her about this book. Better still, why not buy her a copy as a gift? It could be the most valuable gift she's ever received.

APPENDIX 1 – NET WORTH

NAME:				LIABILITIES: what you owe	Liabilities
DATE:					
ASSETS: what you own		Assets			
		£			£
House				Mortgage	
Investment property				Buy to let mortgage	
Investments	ISA 1			Hire purchase 1	
	ISA 2			Hire purchase 2	
	ISA 3			Loan 1	
	ISA 4			Loan 2	
	Unit trust 1			Credit card 1	
	Unit trust 2			Credit card 2	
	Unit trust 3			Credit card 3	
	Stocks and shares 1			Student loan	
	Stocks and shares 2			Overdraft	
	Stocks and shares 3			Owed to family/friends	
Bank account	Account 1				
	Account 2				
	Account 3				
	Account 4				
Premium bonds					
Pension	Pension 1				
	Pension 2				
	Pension 3				
	Pension 4				
Endowments	Endowment 1				
	Endowment 2				
Cash					
TOTAL				**TOTAL**	

Net worth

APPENDIX 2 – INCOME AND EXPENDITURE ANALYSIS

INCOME

NAME: DATE:	MONTH 1	MONTH 2	MONTH 3	AVERAGE
INCOME	£	£	£	£
Salary- net take home				
Self-employed income				
Social security receipts				
Pension				
Investment income e.g. dividends				
Bank interest				
Other:				
TOTAL				

EXPENSES

	MONTH 1	MONTH 2	MONTH 3	AVERAGE
Household expenses	£	£	£	£
Rent				
Electricity				
Gas				
Water rates				
Council tax				
Home telephone				
Mobile telephone				
TV licence				
Digital TV				
Internet				
Alarm				
Buildings insurance				
Contents insurance				
Repairs				
Weekly cleaner				
Monthly gardener				
Groceries				
Alcohol				
Pet foods				
Laundry & dry cleaning				
Other:				
TOTAL				

Children & grandchildren expenses	£	£	£	£
Childcare / baby sitters/nursery				
Clothes & shoes				
Education costs				
After school clubs/activities				
Pocket money				
Other children's expenses				
TOTAL				

Personal expenses	£	£	£	£
Clothes & shoes				
Cigarettes				
Eating out				
Pub/wine bar				
Christmas & birthday presents				
Holidays				
Sports / hobbies				
CD's/books/newspapers				
Travel costs				
Cinema/theatre				
Other personal expenses				
TOTAL				

Motoring expenses	£	£	£	£
Car tax				
Car insurance				
Petrol/diesel				
Servicing & repairs				
Breakdown subscription				
Other motoring expenses				
TOTAL				

Finance costs	£	£	£	£
Mortgage payment				
Hire purchase repayment				
Bank loans repayment				
Bank charges				
Other finance costs:				
TOTAL				

Savings, pension, protection	£	£	£	£
Life assurance premiums	0	0	0	0
Endowment premiums	0	0	0	0
Pension contributions	0	0	0	0
Savings	0	0	0	0
Charitable donations	0	0	0	0
	0	0	0	0
TOTAL	0	0	0	0

CASHFLOW

	MONTH 1	MONTH 2	MONTH 3	AVERAGE
Total income				
Expenses				
Household expenses				
Children & grandchildren expenses				
Personal expenses				
Motoring expenses				
Finance costs				
Savings, pension, protection				
TOTAL EXPENSES				
CASHFLOW				

Your notes

Your notes